Louis Houck
Missouri Historian and Entrepreneur

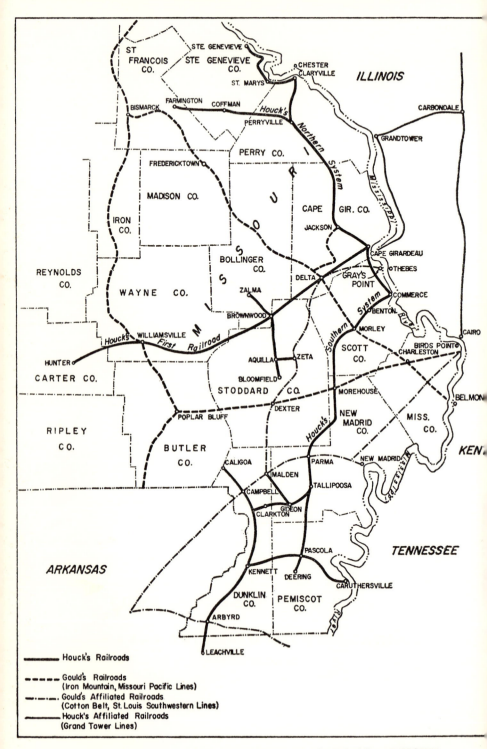

MAP SHOWING EARLY RAILROADS IN SOUTHEAST MISSOURI

Louis Houck

Missouri Historian and

Entrepreneur

William T. Doherty, Jr.

University of Missouri Studies Volume XXXIII

UNIVERSITY OF MISSOURI PRESS
COLUMBIA

TO THE MEMORY OF

Kittie Baird Doherty & William T. Doherty, Sr.

MY MOTHER AND FATHER

PREFACE

William Southern, Jr., Missouri's syndicated columnist, once made a prediction that Louis Houck's "life story would read like a romance. He was a farmer, a statesman, a railroad builder, an author and an historian." This appropriate sentiment was occasioned by memorial services in the spring of 1925 for Southeast Missouri's "indefatigable railroad builder."

A quarter of a century later, John E. Franklin, business partner of Houck, characterized his associate as a "bundle of energy who tried to put some life into the old town of Cape Girardeau." In the penning of his own reminiscences, Franklin was romanticizing the famous Jay Gould-Louis Houck railroad clashes.

Many another had his own version of the versatile Louis Houck's story. All believed that an author of seven books, an editor of seventeen volumes, an entrepreneur responsible for constructing over five hundred railroad miles, was worthy of special study. Faculty and staff of Southeast Missouri State College, Cape Girardeau, Missouri, who assisted the writer in pulling together the threads of Houck's diversified career were the late Miss Sadie Trezevant Kent, librarian emerita; the late Professor William T. Doherty, Sr., chairman of the history department; and the late Dr. W. W. Parker, president of the College.

Of greater significance to the study were the following Houck associates: Major Giboney Houck, Louis Houck's son;

Fred and George Naeter, owners and publishers of the *Cape Girardeau Southeast Missourian;* Mrs. Clarence Walworth Alvord of Columbia, Missouri, and Mrs. Christine Wheeler Heil of Cape Girardeau, Missouri, research assistants to Louis Houck.

Historians of the University of Missouri who critically studied the manuscript were: Dr. Elmer Ellis, president; Dr. Thomas A. Brady, dean of Extra-divisional Administration; Dr. W. Francis English, dean of the College of Arts and Science; and the late Professor Jesse E. Wrench, formerly of the department of history. Particularly, Dr. Lewis E. Atherton, professor of history and chairman of the department, encouraged the author; his efforts and patience far exceeded the duties of professorial advisor.

Dr. James W. Silver, professor of history, and Mrs. Marie Graham Williford, secretary to the Dean of the Graduate School, University of Mississippi, helped in the preparation of the final draft. The University of Mississippi's Committee on Faculty Research provided financial assistance.

Special mention goes to my wife, Dorothy Huff Doherty, without whose interest and cooperation the manuscript might well have wanted completion.

Credit is due to those mentioned above. Defects are solely those of the author.

WILLIAM T. DOHERTY, JR.

University of Mississippi

TABLE OF CONTENTS

Chapter I

THE MAN AND THE WOLF IN THE SWAMPS: ECONOMIC MOTIVATION

"I commenced to build that railroad and after I began to build it I was like the man that caught the wolf. I had the road and it was dangerous to let it go and dangerous to hold on."—Louis Houck, *Statements and Testimony of Railroad Managers* (Jefferson City, Missouri, 1887), p. 347.

WHEN Louis Houck died in 1925, Missouri newspapers, periodicals, societies, and citizens titled him "Empire Builder" and "Missouri's Foremost Historian." This much-honored and multi-careered Missourian was not, however, a native of the state. He was born on April 1, 1840, at Mascoutah, St. Clair County, Illinois, to immigrant parents. His father, Bartholomeaus Houck, born on St. Bartholomew's day in August, 1805, at Hedingsford, near Wurtzburg, Bavaria, was a weaver's son and an architect's grandson, and was himself a journalist. Louis Houck's mother, Kathein Seen, who was of Villegen, canton of Argau, Switzerland, had arrived in the United States in 1828. Her first husband, named Deppler, died of cholera on a journey from New Orleans to St. Louis; she married Bartholomeaus Houck in St. Louis in 1837.

The father of Louis Houck represented the American immigrant saga.[1] At the age of fourteen, Bartholomeaus was apprenticed to learn the arts of printing. For seven years the young man served without salary. In addition, his family subscribed seven hundred florins to secure his career. Within the next eight years, he traversed the European continent in practice of his expensively acquired skill. Landing in Baltimore in 1830, he found railroad work; three years later he moved to Cincinnati. Still drifting westward, to St. Louis, Missouri, Bartholomeaus Houck finally expended his tech-

1

nical knowledge upon a German newspaper, the *Anzieger des Westens*. By 1845 he had advanced to publisher of the *Stern des Westens* at Quincy, Illinois; in 1847-48 he edited in St. Louis the *St. Louiser Zeitung* and *Cosmopolite;* in 1849 he founded the *Belleviller Zeitung,* which he owned and conducted until 1857; and in 1859 he published the first German newspaper in Kansas.[2]

It was natural that Louis Houck labored in his father's printing offices in Belleville, Illinois, mastered the family trade, and became an observer of men and events which made history in the decade before the Civil War. Because the German voters held the balance of power in the frontier states, first between Whigs and Democrats, and later between Republicans and Democrats, young Houck witnessed in his father's printing establishment a regular procession of major Illinois politicians who needed propaganda articles translated into German.[3] Of all office seekers who patronized the printing shop in the 1850's, the one who exercised commanding influence upon young Houck was John Reynolds. He was then working on his *Pioneer History of Illinois* and later, in his own state of "active idleness," he printed in Belleville his autobiography.[4] Unquestionably this fourth governor of Illinois stimulated Houck's interest in early territorial history as well as in genealogical pursuits.

Although Louis Houck's formal education was subsidized by his parents, it was none too regular. In Quincy, Illinois, young Houck attended a Catholic school; in Belleville, Illinois, the German Evangelical school; and at one time his father sent him to Hermann, Missouri, to obtain special instruction in German from a volatile newspaperman, Emil Muehl. Through Muehl, Houck acquired an interest in the serial stories which German newspapers published on their first pages. "These articles," commented the future Missouri chronicler, "were mostly historical and I think by reading the different serials and keeping their plots in mind, I unconsciously trained my memory and also thus acquired a taste for historical reading."[5] Particularly did Houck remember one serial story published in Muehl's paper: "Uncle Tom's Cabin."

At age seventeen, young Houck disposed of his share of the publishing interests for $800 and departed for the University of Wisconsin, primarily because he spoke English "indifferently."[6] His funds enabled him to devote one year and three months to the study of English, German, Latin, and Greek.

In 1859 Houck returned to Illinois exhibiting political sympathies with the Democrats and most definitely divorcing himself from those Germans who favored the new Republican party. William R. Morrison, Speaker of the House, and later an original member of the Interstate Commerce Commission, induced Houck to start a German newspaper, the *Volksblatt*, in Belleville, Illinois, in the interest of the Democratic party. Houck acquiesced, and expanded his political propagandizing with orations in German in his home community, in southern Illinois, and in Indiana. In 1863 he was rewarded by being made enrolling and engrossing clerk of the Illinois General Assembly prorogued by Republican Governor Richard Yates.[7]

Houck admitted that when the Civil War came on, "I was not very enthusiastically in favor of the war and became very unpopular on account of my opposition to Lincoln."[8] This unpopularity came to a climax on May 10, 1864, when an armed mob of soldiers destroyed the printing establishment of the *Volksblatt*. In an article addressed to patrons of his paper, Houck indignantly reported that his father had been injured, the office wrecked, and that an appeal to the law had proved hopeless. Defiantly Houck proclaimed:

> It is thus that in all ages, and in all countries, the advocates of despotism attempt to silence free speech and free press, and those worshipping at the altar of their country's freedom. It is thus that the advocates of American despotism have been attempting, during the last three years, to silence those opposing their wicked and nefarious schemes. They cannot silence us. We will talk. We have survived the first destruction of our office — we

will survive the second. We will yet live to see
the patriot mask torn from the faces of northern
disunionists and traitors. For that end we labor.
Our cause will triumph. We know we are right and
will advocate the right. We have done so during
the last three years—we will do so in the future.
The *Volksblatt* will soon reappear. Only for a few
weeks we ask the indulgence of our readers.[9]

Unrelentingly, Houck's paper continued its attack on usurpa-
tion of congressional authority by Abraham Lincoln. With
biting sarcasm, the editor criticized Illinois Germans hired
to enter Missouri to break its Confederate sympathy.

In addition to political editorializing, Houck, in his
personal columns, was discovering for himself and his readers
a useful philosophy of American life for after the war.
Houck reasoned:

The scholar, the capitalist, the artisan, are alike
employed. What would life be without some occupa-
tion? Would men be happy? No. Idleness, the root
of vice, is the evil spirit which embitters the life
of the rich and wealthy, who disdains both manual
and intellectual work.

In behalf of his own "industrious" theme, Louis Houck
studied law, was admitted to the Illinois bar, and never
abandoned his scholarly research and writing. The first of
his legal treatises, an abstract of all state statutes and judicial
opinions rendered on mechanics liens, was published in 1866[10]
and dedicated to another Illinois historian, Sidney Breese.
A Treatise on the Law of Navigable Rivers, an expansion of
an article accepted earlier by the *American Law Review*, was
issued in 1868.[11] Thus Houck learned one major historical
maxim: to precede book publication by article publication.
Perhaps he discovered yet another *nuda veritas* of scholarly
production when he commented, "Of course, I made no money
out of my books but they were a very great intellectual
benefit to me."[12] Actually, his first works had been undertaken pragmatically because of difficulty experienced in securing technical data necessary in the handling of private
litigation.

Moving from Cairo, Illinois, to St. Louis, Missouri, in 1868, Houck procured the position of Assistant United States District Attorney.[13] A publication career was assured when Houck became correspondent of the *Missouri Republican* under the *nom de plume*, "Ariel."[14] As columnist, he interpreted decisions of the Supreme Court, contributed miscellaneous articles on diverse topics such as the significance of historic names of towns in southern Illinois, reviewed literary works, and translated foreign compositions. Resigning his St. Louis post at the time U. S. Grant entered the White House, Houck never seriously considered politics as a career thereafter. He was convinced that "no one has any chance to wield any influence or accomplish anything unless supported with ample sums of money or a combination of political managers."[15] Without such aids it seemed to Houck that man was a mere cipher, and, what was more pertinent, "my experience as a salaried officer created a great prejudice in my mind against working for a salary."

Believing in 1869 that a "move from a city to the country would enable an individual to wield greater influence and accomplish more," Houck arrived in Cape Girardeau, Missouri,[16] which then had 2,700 inhabitants, two-thirds German. Originally a French colony on the Mississippi River, this settlement was old enough in Louisiana territorial history to possess sufficient lore for the future historian of the state.

Within the first year of residence, Louis Houck annotated fifteen volumes of the *Missouri Reports*.[17] As the project was subsidized by the state, Houck for the first, as well as the last time, realized financial profits from scholarship. In addition, he attracted attention to himself as a young man of competence. When the *Reports* appeared, the *Missouri Republican* favorably commented:

> The editor and compiler has exhibited a thorough acquaintance with the necessities of practice in this arrangement, and great pains and labor are evident in the thoroughness and completeness with which he has performed his task. His notes are also in evidence of his general legal knowledge and superior qualifications for the work.[18]

Kindly reviews were gratifying, but of immediate importance to Houck was the ability to make ready references to these decisions in the courtroom. Houck's agility as a scholar helped establish his legal reputation within the state.

Because of his new residence, Houck's association with the *Missouri Republican* as a correspondent was modified. In his news dispatches he assumed the role of propagandist for the southeastern section of the state. The young journalist may have sometimes appeared hard pressed for items that would attract settlers into the bootheel of Missouri, as when he wrote about the spacious campus of St. Vincent's Academy at Cape Girardeau, but such items demonstrated his advertising ability. Houck permitted himself to wonder in this dispatch "why so many young men should shut themselves up in the strait and narrow enclosures of city universities, and not rather seek the ample grounds and pure atmosphere of a county retreat of learning, like St. Vincent's College."[19]

"The 'cape' has always been a pleasant place," he reported.[20] "Before the war the 'belles' of the cape were famous, nor are they unsung since the war." On Christmas day, 1872, Louis Houck married one of the belles, Mary Hunter Giboney, only child of an important landowner, whose property was originally a substantial Spanish land grant of 1798. Consequently, Louis Houck became more interested in Cape Girardeau's real estate values, which had been seriously affected by the railroad debt then hanging over the town. Successful railroad building was Houck's chief solution to the problem of increasing property values from the 1870's to the turn of the century.

On April 1, 1870, Houck, in the role of newspaper correspondent, dismally summarized for his metropolitan readers the economic plight of the agrarian, swampy, southeastern section of the state of Missouri:

> Business here, as everywhere else, I suppose, is dull. Money is scarce—scarcer than the mythical "oldest inhabitant" can remember; but we all live in hope of a better future.[21]

Tomorrow's prosperity, reasoned Houck, could be provided in part by advertising resources of the region, which
would in turn attract prospective inhabitants. Since settlers
had avoided southeast Missouri for one paramount reason,
its swamps, an advertisement that Dunklin County was not
subject to droughts demonstrated Houck's talent for propaganda.[22] According to the early theme, reiterated years later
in Houck's state histories,[23] the southeastern section of the
state surpassed every other portion of Missouri in fertility
of soil, variety of mineral resources, and mildness and
salubrity of climate. In essence, land was not only cheaper,
but was better in the Missouri bootheel than elsewhere.[24]

Town by town, Houck, as roving reporter, singled out
unique economic advantages. In Charleston, Missouri, "the
finest garden vegetables grow with little labor and of better
quality than in southern Illinois; here the acre yields 80 to
125 bushels of corn; and leaf tobacco and the finest grains
can be grown." At New Madrid, Missouri, readers were informed the corn crop had never failed, and that fields which
for twenty-five years had been planted with corn annually
yielded forty bushels per acre.

County by county, Louis Houck enumerated natural
resources of the southeastern section. "Dunklin has finer
cotton lands, New Madrid better corn lands, Madison and
Iron more mineral wealth," he wrote, "but in Stoddard you
find at once cotton, corn, and wheat lands. . . ." However,
in viewing the area as a whole, the striking thing Houck
noticed was the abundance of timber. Having ridden through
magnificent forests of oak, gum, and elm, as well as beech,
ash, and poplar, Houck came to the not unreasonable conclusion that here lay "a source of great wealth."

Not by his writing alone did Houck present his vision
of the growing economic importance of the bootheel section
of the state. In a speech, "The resources and future of southeast Missouri," delivered at Fredericktown, Missouri, on
September 28, 1869, Houck outlined certain steps necessary

to bring prosperity to the area: formation of immigration
societies in every southeastern county of Missouri, building
of railroads, improvement of rivers, development of mineral
wealth, and appropriation of a half million acres for a national school of mines within the region.[25]

The thirty year old promoter also expressed political
viewpoints which buttressed, in his mind, the future economic
well-being of the section which was to be his home for the
next half century. National, state, and local governments
must be liberal in their aid of internal improvements. Rivers
must be improved, and builders of railroads adequately subsidized for their labors. At the same time, however, other
types of government aid were wrong. On October 21, 1869,
he wrote the *Missouri Republican* that "while everything the
farmer needs, plows, harrows, clothing, etc., is very high,
owing to the unjust and outrageous tariffs, all the productions
of the soil sell at ridiculously low figures." Such a situation,
Houck contended, was due to unjust Radical legislation which
fostered every interest at expense of the great West. In an
address titled "Monopolies" delivered in March, 1870, the
future historian of Missouri anticipated the Beardian thesis
that the Civil War was a second American revolution; the
recent conflict appeared to Houck as gigantic Eastern
speculation which

> has virtually given the capitalists a mortgage lien
> on the real and personal property of the nation.
> The 14th amendment, the reconstruction measures
> of Congress, the elevation of the negro to a position
> to which he is utterly unfit, have all been effected
> to permanently secure the dominion of the manu-
> facturing over the agricultural interest—the East
> over the West and the South.[26]

In similar vein was his speech, "The Tendency to Centralization," delivered at Charleston, Missouri, on July 27,
1872. Describing the federal system as one which simultaneously secured national unity and state sovereignty, Houck
severely denounced federal interference in state affairs as a
perversion of the original constitutional principles; the

recently passed Ku Klux act and supervision of state elections were inadmissable. Houck thought that the best possible political remedy at the time was to elect Greeley, adopt a one-term principle for the Presidency, and secure a liberal Democratic House of Representatives.

Propagandizing, advertising, and political action, however, Houck eventually bequeathed to others. For twelve years, 1869-1881, he pondered the advisability of undertaking railroad construction as a means of promoting prosperity; then, not unexpectedly, he began to practice what he had preached. The process of Houck's conversion from law and journalism to an active railroad career in the Mid-west is suggestive of the transformation undergone by substantial New England railroad men in the same period of American history as described by Edward Chase Kirkland in his study, *Men, Cities and Transportation.*[27]

Louis Houck had been in Cape Girardeau, Missouri, only four months in 1869 when he reported to the *Missouri Republican* that railroad projects in southeast Missouri were advisable and that every community desired a railroad. He scolded, however, that "while the northern portion of the State has been pushing ahead improvements of this character, Southeast Missouri slept the sleep of Rip Van Winkle."[28]

The reporting was not accurate. Actually, southeast Missouri was experiencing railroad construction, which on the face of a Missouri map assumed triangular shape.[29] The St. Louis and Iron Mountain Railroad had been completed from St. Louis to Ironton before 1860 and was being projected south to Helena, Arkansas, to assume a perpendicular side of a triangle. The Cairo and Fulton Railroad, moving from Cairo on the Mississippi River westward toward Poplar Bluff, Missouri, had proceeded more than half its distance before the Civil War to form the base of the triangle. When the Cairo and Fulton, and the St. Louis and Iron Mountain had been jointly purchased in 1867, and the intersection of the two roads completed in September, 1873, the triangle became even more of an actuality. In 1868, an extension of the Iron

Mountain from Bismarck, a few miles north of Ironton, to Belmont, on the Mississippi River, formed the hypotenuse of the triangle and closed it in by crossing the Cairo and Fulton road at Charleston. In 1880 the above property was brought under the control of the Gould mid-western railroad interests.[30]

Instead of southeast Missouri being completely neglected, it was, of course, Houck's new home that was left outside the pattern of railroad construction. Other towns of southeast Missouri, according to Houck's predictions, were to become the beneficiaries of Cape Girardeau's once pre-eminent trading position. For example, he wrote from Charleston, Missouri, when the Iron Mountain entered that town: "It is of course useless to expatiate on the utility of a railroad. Everybody knows that a railroad is a good institution. It will make this county the garden of vegetables for St. Louis and Chicago."[31]

From Fredericktown, Missouri, he wrote his estimate that the population of that town doubled as a consequence of Iron Mountain completion.[32]

The city of Cape Girardeau, prodded by Houck's reporting, considered attaching as well as intersecting the railroad triangle. The Cape Girardeau and State Line Railroad was chartered; it was designed to cross the Iron Mountain's Belmont branch about two miles below Allenville, and then proceed in a southwesterly direction over the area encompassed by the triangle to the Arkansas state line.[33] On April 1, 1870, Houck enthusiastically supported the proposed line by calling attention to certain significant factors.[34] The road would originate at one of the largest shipping points on the Mississippi River. Cape Girardeau was in close proximity to the Big Muddy coal fields to the north. Because the road was a down-grade run from Allenville to Cape Girardeau, this line could ship, with the same motive power, twice as much ore as the Iron Mountain could ship elsewhere. As the region through which the line passed contained iron, Houck concluded that Cape Girardeau would undoubtedly become a "Pittsburgh of the West." This complemented an earlier prediction that his home town's destiny was to be a manufacturing city.[35]

Despite such ingenious arguments advanced to obtain support of the project, Cape Girardeau's early hope of rail connection was shattered. Officers of the road failed to procure additional capital other than by local subscription.[36] The construction company, having laid only four miles of track and graded some forty miles, suspended operation in the panic year of 1873.[37] Unfortunately for Cape Girardeau, officials had increased the city's railroad indebtedness by joining into the mortgages of the construction company's other railroad properties to the tune of one and one-half million dollars.[38] According to Houck's law partner, the business of the city was thereby paralyzed for the next eight years because of the existing railroad debt.[39] As a consequence, he reported, men of capital avoided the river town, citizens who had money kept it hidden, and real estate values fell until property could scarcely be sold. In the years immediately following the 1873 panic, Cape Girardeau, like many another western town, even one with a completed railroad, was undergoing depression due to its railroad debt. According to the historian of the western railroads, these town and county debts were even more objectionable than state debts. They were more immediate, and larger in proportion to the total wealth of the citizen body.[40]

At this critical juncture Louis Houck became actively involved in the destiny of Cape Girardeau's unfinished railroad. His legal services were procured to disentangle property of the Cape road from the construction company's mortgages. In addition to this case, successfully completed in 1878, Houck was responsible for a bill introduced in the Missouri legislature which provided that two-thirds of the amounts collected on saloon licenses of the city be applied to payment of interest as well as to reduction of the city's railroad debt.[41] Thus Houck's initial involvement with railroads was in the capacity of lawyer, the profession characterized by Kirkland as *de luxe* training for railroading careers in the latter part of the nineteenth century.[42]

When a new company, the Cape Girardeau Railway Company, was incorporated on August 10, 1880, in place of the old, Houck appeared in the capacity of president and railroad director.[43] In his testimony before a legislative committee in 1887 Houck succinctly described his entrance into the transportation field:

> Public opinion, to a certain extent, and my own inclinations, being a large property holder in that territory, compelled me to take hold of that enterprise in order to secure and afford our town its benefits as well as develop the material resources of that section.[44]

He recalled that before he assumed active control "we interviewed capitalists, we offered them the money we had invested . . . we tried to get foreign capitalists to build it. We wrote letters in every direction." But as there were no results, he concluded the job was his.

Certain other considerations obviously attracted Houck. The new company received title to all property of the old road when and if by January 1, 1881, Houck completed his line from Cape Girardeau to the Iron Mountain system, a distance of 14.4 miles.[45] Houck was assured of a subscription list and a personal bonus of $10,000 if the road was completed in given time.[46] As time drew short, the number of ties used in the construction diminished to one-half, then one-fourth of the standard number required.[47] For building of trestles, timber was procured alongside the roadbed and "no question was asked who owned the timber or land, for everybody wanted the railroad."[48] Houck was so short of rail at the end of construction that in order to get into the city on time he had to tear up several hundred feet of rail laid behind in order to build ahead.[49] But in compliance with his contract, Houck had tied his city to a transportation outlet. He had also involved himself in the railroad game, an association which lasted from January 1, 1881, until his death in 1925.

The fourteen mile extension completed by 1881 only whetted Houck's appetite for more construction. For the next forty years Houck repeated the process of building "feeders" to major "through lines" in southeast Missouri. He was never engaged in construction which put him at any great distance from these "through lines" or from another natural outlet, the Mississippi River. Yet in the slow process of adding sections to sections, Houck, by 1891, had completed a hundred mile railroad which traversed the Iron Mountain triangular system in southern Missouri and was presumably headed for Fort Smith, Arkansas. From 1892 to 1902 he created a second network, approximating 250 miles of line, south of Cape Girardeau. This southern network intertwined once again the Iron Mountain and also the St. Louis Southwestern, better known as the Cotton Belt, and was destined for Memphis. With St. Louis as the evident terminus, Louis Houck also organized and constructed from 1893 to 1913 a network north of Cape Girardeau. Thus Houck had at one time or another engaged in the construction of three systems which comprised some 500 miles in southeast Missouri and had also undertaken unsuccessfully the promotion of certain lines in southern Illinois with which he could tie his systems to a possible Chicago outlet. In short, he valiantly struggled to move north, south, east, and west from his Mississippi River terminus, Cape Girardeau.

Was this short-line railroad builder motivated only by his well-publicized public-spirited aim to free his home town from the isolation caused by lack of transportation facilities? Although evidence of Houck's objectives in building every section of his railroad is not available, there is evidence that certain motives other than enlightened civic interest must be considered in any study of the "Empire Builder" who "has certainly done more for South East Missouri than any fifteen men, and if he has prospered, we have all prospered with him."[50] A study of Houck's involved litigation, always one of his chief activities as a short-line railroad builder, indicates that he expected rewards from such litigation.

Louis Houck was motivated, in part, by the hope of obtaining county land subsidies. Concerning the 1851 congressional grant of swamp lands to the state and the state of Missouri's grant of the lands to the counties, Louis Houck had earlier written:

> On the whole it may be said that the grant has been a curse to us—a never-failing fountain of rascality and a source of corruption. Our plain and unsophisticated county courts became a prey to the wiley snares of sharpers who, as soon as they perceived that the county judges became the dispensers of wide and lordly domains, began to "make friends" with them, and thus to establish their claims to official consideration.[51]

At first glance it would seem that Houck, who was a courtroom sophisticate, could expect no grants. Short-line railroad directors who built in the late nineteenth century, when such subsidies were rapidly coming to an end, could anticipate few favors. This seemed particularly true since farmers and other taxpayers blamed the 1873 depression upon railroads. As a result, Missouri's Constitutional Convention of 1875 declared all further county aid illegal.[52] Nevertheless, as the Houck litigation attests, the Missourian proceeded in his railroad career as if he were at work in an earlier historical era.

In one of the extensions to his first railroad, Houck coupled construction with the draining of Mingo Bottom in Wayne County. In contract with the county, Louis Houck agreed to build a levee twelve miles long over which his railroad would pass, to cut away the timber on either side of the levee, and to construct necessary drains and ditches. In return for such reclamation work, Wayne County would deed 10,000 acres of its swamp lands to the Cape Girardeau railroad director. To the *Missouri Republican*, Wayne County appeared to be getting a railroad "cheaply enough" because "it is said that the lands Mr. Houck gets are, during a portion of the year, under water, and that to reclaim them the beds of the river which are higher than that of 'mingo swamp' in which the lands are located, must be lowered."[53] However, the paper's statement, "it is not likely that he will suffer by his undertaking," was an overestimate.

The St. Louis newspaper badly miscalculated the extent of Houck's rewards. First, the state board of education petitioned the Missouri Supreme Court for cancellation of Houck's contract, claiming that swamp land payments were earmarked for school funds.[54] The court ruled that county courts had power to sell swamp lands and that the school fund was entitled only to surpluses remaining after expenses of reclamation had been paid. Houck, of course, had no objection to such ruling. But in a second case,[55] as Houck's contract was "merely a donation of the lands to the company in consideration of building and operating its road, and not a contract to deed swamp lands as payment for reclaiming them," the Supreme Court declared that the county court had exceeded its powers of negotiation with Houck and hence voided the railroad company's contract. To the state's highest tribunal, provisions of the contract amounted "to this and no more":

> The company agrees to dig ditches along the sides of the railroad embankment, so as to drain water into such openings as the company sees fit to make. This is no more than an embankment built for railroad purposes only would require. The law requires every railroad company to make such drains along the sides of its roads. . . . It does not make this embankment a levee to call it by that name.[56]

Houck was persistent. Compelled to employ new parties in his litigation in order to gain renewed consideration before the Supreme Court, he was rebuffed twice more because justices saw no differences between the later cases and the original one.[57] These decisions simply demonstrated Houck's litigious nature and his obstinancy regarding benefits due a railroad builder.

Because his claim for a land bonus had been thrice disposed of in connection with his first railroad, it is somewhat surprising to discover Houck trying for an even larger land bonus when he added one of his railroad sections to his second network of roads. The *St. Louis Globe-Democrat* reported September 15, 1891, that Louis Houck would receive 40,000 acres of land from Pemiscot County for the construction of a line from Kennett, Missouri, to Caruthersville, Missouri. For good measure another paper added:

> Hurrah for Pemiscot County!
> Hurrah for Louis Houck!
> Poor Mr. Gould: he is not in it![58]

The editor commented on the local setting for the railroad in a manner reminiscent of the earlier Houck journalism:

> This road will be a paying one from the start, for the simple reason that the entire line is built through a section of the country, the soil of which is as fertile as the far famed valley of the Nile, and the portion that is in cultivation yields immense crops of corn, cotton, potatoes, and in fact everything the farmer chooses to grow; while the unimproved land is covered with an enormous growth of the most valuable timber, which will be converted into lumber by a number of fine saw mills soon to be erected along the line of the road.

Newspapers had perhaps discovered the quid-pro-quo arrangements, but had not been over-concerned with technicalities of the contract.[59] First, Louis Houck purchased the land at $1.25 an acre, securing his note with bonds of the railroad as collateral. Then in a contract between Houck and the county—not a contract between a railroad and a county as it had been in the Mingo Swamp deal—Houck agreed to build a railroad and dig a ditch along side of the road which would divert the water into two natural drainage channels. If the railroad and ditch were completed on time, the note would be returned by the county to Houck; if he failed to finish the construction, he would deed the 40,000 acres back to Pemiscot County.

His business partner, to whom he had promised half the land bonus as well as half the bonds of the railroad company in return for cash needed in the immediate construction task, reasoned:

> This land deal looked to me like an evasion of the law, and it occurred to me that if I joined Houck I might ultimately have to pay the county $1.25 an acre for my share of the land in order to obtain a perfect title. I figured however that the building of the railroad and completion of the levee would so increase the value of Pemiscot County land that I could afford to take the risk.[60]

When Pemiscot County not unexpectedly threatened suit for recovery of its lands after completion of both railroad and levee, Houck "walked up and down the floor asserting that he would have his lawyers fight the damn rascals in the courts and establish the soundness of our title to the lands."[61] But remembering the Mingo Swamp fiasco, cooler heads prevailed and the final settlement was not rendered by courts. Houck gave his partner a quitclaim deed to the land, realizing fifty cents per acre, and Franklin offered to pay the county $1.25 an acre if the money was expended for drainage purposes. Houck, Franklin, and the county were thus satisfied.

In spite of Houck's belief that levee building could easily be coupled with railroad construction, the Missouri railway commission's reports suggested that Houck's building was no more designed to be of permanent nature than was his reclamation work. In 1891, in a survey of Houck's first enterprise, commissioners reported sixty out of ninety-five miles laid with shattered, splintered, twisted, old, worn-out rails; many trestles and culverts in shaky condition; and the line badly in need of ditching.[62] One person picturesquely remembered his southern system:

> The road was known locally as the "peavine," because it was so crooked, and sometimes for days at a time there would be no trains, because the one

engine and coach would jump the track. . . . At one
place just south of Benton, Houck had felled two
trees and laid them across a small creek, building his
track on this structure instead of the regulation
trestle. This caused the track to rise up in order to
get on the trestle, and we recall the warning which
the conductor always gave the passengers: "Look
out, she's going to jump!" in order that they might
prepare themselves for the sudden change in the
level of the roadbed.[63]

Officials reported his northern system as follows:

It is badly out of repair its entire length of 43
miles. . . . The rails are badly warped and bent and
out of alignment. Some of the rails are broken and
patched, and some are without any support whatever, and there are broken angle bars almost without
number; many of the angle bars are fastened to the
rail with one bolt, there being no hole through the
rail to permit of the use of a bolt in the other end
of the bar. . . . The cuts, without exception, are in
deplorable condition, so much so that it is almost
impossible for trains to get through them.[64]

Years later, Houck, the amateur railroad builder who
had identified jerry-type railroad construction with levee
building, and who could not quite comprehend changes in
climate of opinion wrought by the Populist and Progressive
eras in American history, became an opponent of the Little
River Drainage District charged with reclamation work in
southeast Missouri. Houck, as litigation attests, was as un-
convinced about the propriety of engineered drainage at
taxpayers' expense as he had been unconcerned about new
regulatory railroad legislation demanded by the American
public following Reconstruction. The cases of Houck versus
the drainage districts turned out to be "One of those typical
Houck suits fought for all it is worth and taken from one
court to another until the highest bench in the land is reached
for a final decision, unless Louis Houck can discover someway
of getting it over to the Hague."[65]

The *St. Louis Republic*, taking cognizance of the clash
of opinion between "the immediate interests of the builder
of small railroads" and the agrarians, reasoned:

The small railroad builder in Southeast Missouri perforce employs cheap methods of construction in order to reap an immediate harvest from the tonnage of logs and lumber. He is usually also an owner of timbered lands. Drainage schemes, like irrigation projects, are expensive. He might naturally be inclined to hold his land for the appreciation in value of the standing timber, or cut and ship the timber, and then wait for the swamp land, worth little and costing but little in taxes, to rise slowly in price. On this scene enters the agriculturist, a man to whom a farm is a bigger thing than a sawmill, and a carload of peaches or watermelons than a carload of cypress shingles.[66]

Considering the physical conditions of southeast Missouri in the late nineteenth century, a section long known in the twentieth century as "Swamp-East Missouri," it was not surprising that Houck treated railroad construction and reclamation as coordinated extractive industries. It was characteristic of the *laissez-faire* philosophy which dominated the United States following the Civil War that a lawyer-journalist, who was only accidentally a railroad builder, should utilize the courts in his efforts to obtain what he considered his natural rewards for the economic improvement of a city, a section, and a state.

NOTES TO CHAPTER I

[1] Louis Houck, "Reminiscences" [Cape Girardeau, Missouri, n.d., n.p.]. See also B. A. Beinlich, "The Latin Immigration to Illinois," *Transactions of the Illinois State Historical Society*, No. 14 (1909), pp. 209-14, and Oswald Garrison Villard, "The 'Latin Peasants' of Belleville, Illinois," *Journal of the Illinois State Historical Society*, XXXV (March, 1942), 7.

[2] Unidentified news clippings [n.d.] on death of B. Houck, three in German, one in English, pasted in scrapbook of Louis Houck, Cape Girardeau, Missouri. Also see Franklin William Scott, "Newspapers and Periodicals of Illinois, 1814-1879," *Collections of the Illinois State Historical Library*, VI (Springfield, Illinois, 1910), 21-23, 291.

[3] Arthur C. Cole, *The Era of the Civil War, 1848-1870* (Springfield, Illinois, 1919), p. 62, and Thomas J. McCormack, editor, *Memoirs of Gustav Koerner*, I (Cedar Rapids, 1909), 549-50.

[4] John Reynolds, *The Pioneer History of Illinois* (Belleville, Illinois, 1852). This work covers the period from discovery in 1673

to 1818, the year when the state government of Illinois was organized. Similarly Houck's history is "from the earliest explorations and settlements until the admission of the state into the union." Also see John Reynolds, *My Own Times, embracing also, the History of My Life* (Belleville, Illinois, 1855), p. 595.

Giboney Houck, Louis Houck's son, stated that Reynolds was a major influence upon his father. Interview, Cape Girardeau, Missouri, summer, 1950.

[5] Houck, "Reminiscences," pp. 24-25. Also see William G. Bek, *The German Settlement Society of Philadelphia and Its Colony, Hermann, Missouri* (Philadelphia, 1907), pp. 128-145; William G. Bek, "The Followers of Duden," *Missouri Historical Review,* XVII (October, 1922), 54.

[6] *Ibid.* p. 26. Also see the *11th Annual Report of the University of Wisconsin* (1858), Appendix E, p. 53; Merle Curti and Vernon Carstensen, *The University of Wisconsin, A History, 1848-1925,* I (Madison, Wisconsin, 1949), 187.

[7] *Journal of the Senate of the 23rd General Assembly of Illinois* (Springfield, Illinois, 1863), pp. 4, 393-5.

[8] Houck, "Reminiscences," p. 29.

[9] Clipping from *Volksblatt* (Belleville, Illinois), May 20, 1864, in scrapbook of Louis Houck [Cape Girardeau, Missouri, n.d.].

[10] Louis Houck, *A Treatise on the Mechanics Lien Law in the United States* (Chicago, 1867). Like Reynolds, Breese was a historian as well as a railroad builder. See Sidney Breese, *The Early History of Illinois* (Chicago, 1844). Like Houck, Breese was also first official reporter of the Supreme Court of Illinois and issued its first volume of decisions, as Houck was to do later with his *Missouri Reports.*

[11] Louis Houck, "Navigable Rivers," *American Law Review,* II (1868), 589-98; Louis Houck, *A Treatise on the Law of Navigable Rivers* (Boston, 1868).

[12] Houck, "Reminiscences," p. 33.

[13] Louis Houck served under General John W. Noble. Noble was later employed by Houck in several of his railroad controversies. In the Benjamin Harrison administration, Noble served as Secretary of the Interior. See *Missouri Republican* (St. Louis, Missouri), December 4, 1868, and *The Bench and Bar of St. Louis, Kansas City, Jefferson City, and other Missouri Cities* (St. Louis, 1888).

[14] At the time Houck was employed by the *Republican,* it "consistently antagonized all measures of doubtful constitutionality on the part of the Lincoln administration and it was owing to its utterances and influences, steadily and persistently exerted, that the 'bolt' in the Republican party which led to the election of B. Gratz Brown as Governor was organized and consummated." J. Thomas Scharf, *History of St. Louis City and County,* I (Philadelphia, 1883), 918. In later years Houck used the name "Ariel" for an historical account of the Sturdivant Bank of Cape Girardeau, Missouri, in the *Missouri Historical Review,* XVII (July, 1923), 522-4.

[15] Houck, "Reminiscences," p. 49.

[16] *Missouri Republican,* May 3, 1869.

[17] Louis Houck (ed.), *Reports of Cases argued and determined in the Supreme Court of the State of Missouri from 1835 to 1837* (15 vols., Belleville, Illinois, 1870). Also see *Laws of the State of Missouri, passed at the Adjourned Session of the 25th General Assembly* (Jefferson City, 1870), p. 113. The state of Missouri was required to purchase 300 copies of the set, and Louis Houck was to furnish each volume at not more than $2.60. A sum of $11,000 was appropriated for this purpose.

[18] *Missouri Republican,* September 24, 1870.

[19] *Missouri Republican,* July 5, 1869.

[20] *Ibid.,* December 2, 1869. Also see *Southeast Missourian* (Cape Girardeau, Missouri), December 21, 1944 (Obituary of Mrs. Louis Houck), and Louis Houck, *Memorial Sketches of Pioneers and Early Residents of Southeast Missouri* (Cape Girardeau, Missouri, 1915), p. 77.

[21] *Missouri Republican,* April 1, 1870.

[22] *Ibid.,* September 17, 1869.

[23] Louis Houck, *A History of Missouri,* I (Chicago, 1908), 31-32.

[24] *Missouri Republican,* 1869, *passim.*

[25] In Louis Houck's scrapbook, titled "Articles by Louis Houck", [Cape Girardeau, Missouri, n.d., n.p.].

[26] *Ibid.*

[27] Edward Chase Kirkland, *Men, Cities, and Transportation,* II (Cambridge, 1948), 454-74.

[28] *Missouri Republican,* August 12, 1869.

[29] See maps in Margaret Louise Fitzsimmons, "Railroad Development in Missouri, 1860 to 1870" (unpublished Master's thesis, Washington University, St. Louis, Missouri, 1931).

[30] Maynard Cameron Willis, "The Construction of Railroads in Southeast Missouri" (unpublished Master's thesis, University of Missouri, Columbia, Missouri, 1933), pp. 101, 103; John W. Million, *State Aid to Railways in Missouri* (Chicago, 1896), p. 155.

[31] *Missouri Republican,* November 26, 1869.

[32] *Ibid.,* October 1, 1870.

[33] *The Combined 5th and 6th Annual Reports of the Railroad Commissioners of Missouri* (1879 and 1880), p. 14.

[34] *Missouri Republican,* April 1, 1870.

[35] *Ibid.,* December 2, 1869.

[36] *St. Louis Post-Dispatch,* June 1, 1929; and Fitzsimmons, p. 351.

[37] *Combined 5th and 6th Report,* p. 14.

[38] Willis, p. 111.

[39] Robert G. Ranney, "The City's Railroads," *City Directory of Cape Girardeau, Missouri, for 1906* (Cape Girardeau, Missouri, 1906), pp. 198-207.

[40] Robert E. Reigel, *The Story of the Western Railroads* (New York, 1927), p. 137.

22   MISSOURI HISTORIAN AND ENTREPRENEUR

⁴¹ Ranney, p. 200; also see *Cape Girardeau Southeast Missourian,* May 16, 1919.

⁴² Kirkland, pp. 467-68.

⁴³ *Combined 5th and 6th Report,* p. 14.

⁴⁴ *Statements and Testimony of Railroad Managers,* 34th General Assembly of Missouri (Jefferson City, Missouri, 1887), p. 347.

⁴⁵ *Weekly Republican* (Cape Girardeau, Missouri), May 25, 1915.

⁴⁶ Norwin D. Houser, "Louis Houck," ([Pamphlet issued by Southeast Missouri State College] Cape Girardeau, Missouri, October 15, 1949).

⁴⁷ *Weekly Republican,* May 28, 1915.

⁴⁸ Louis Houck, "Railroad Work" (unpublished manuscript, Cape Girardeau, Missouri, in possession of Giboney Houck).

⁴⁹ *Enterprise Courier* (Charleston, Missouri), February 26, 1925.

⁵⁰ *Dunklin Democrat* (Kennett, Missouri), September 13, 1902.

⁵¹ *Missouri Republican,* July 7, 1870.

⁵² Edwin L. Lopata, *Local Aids to Railroads in Missouri* (New York, 1937), p. 130.

⁵³ *Missouri Republican,* March 27, 1882.

⁵⁴ "State *ex rel.* Board of Education, Appellant, vs. the County Court of Wayne County," *Missouri Reports,* IIC (Columbia, Missouri, 1889), pp. 362-8.

⁵⁵ Cape Girardeau Southwestern Railway Company, Appellant, vs. Hatton, *Missouri Reports,* CII (Columbia, Missouri, 1890), pp. 45-46.

⁵⁶ *Missouri Reports,* CII, p. 55.

⁵⁷ "William Brown Estate Company, Appellant, vs. Wayne County," *Missouri Reports,* CXXIII (Columbia, Missouri, 1894), pp. 464-79; "St. Louis, Cape Girardeau and Fort Smith Railway, Appellant, vs. Wayne County," *Missouri Reports,* CXXV (Columbia, Missouri, 1895), pp. 351-8.

⁵⁸ *Cape Girardeau Democrat,* January 5, 1895.

⁵⁹ See John Eddy Franklin memoirs published in *The Democrat Argus* (Caruthersville, Missouri), June 15, 1946, to August 2, 1946.

⁶⁰ *Democrat Argus,* July 5, 1946.

⁶¹ *Ibid.,* July 12, 1946.

⁶² *17th Annual Report of Railroad and Warehouse Commissioners of Missouri,* 1891, p. 280.

⁶³ *Charleston Enterprise Courier* (Charleston, Missouri), February 26, 1925, reprinted in *Missouri Historical Review,* XXI, 133.

⁶⁴ *33rd Annual Report of Railroad and Warehouse Commissioners of Missouri,* 1908, p. 127.

⁶⁵ *Weekly Republican,* October 29, 1915.

⁶⁶ *St. Louis Republic,* July 29, 1911.

Chapter II

ROBBER BARON VERSUS BUZZ-SAW: AN EPISODE IN MISSOURI RAILROAD HISTORY, 1893-1896

"You are the first man that ever beat me in a railroad fight. I have seen your railroads. . . . I have heard you conduct your cases . . . and I want to say, sir, that you are a d— poor railroad man, but a d— fine lawyer."—Jay Gould, as quoted in the *Enterprise Courier*, Charleston, Missouri, February 26, 1925.

THE AVERAGE citizen, the *St. Louis Republic* once stated with reference to Louis Houck's railroad career in southern Missouri, "would do well to think a number of times before becoming tangled up with a small railroad, either in its inception, construction, or operation."[1] The newspaper cautioned that the West and South were replete with evidence of the wreckage and ruin of private fortunes frittered away by useless endeavors and by endless litigation to put through some "jim crow" road. In bristling reply, Houck attacked the "jim crow" inference and forcefully reminded his readers that Gould interests were only too willing to obtain his property.[2]

So it was that from 1893 to 1896 Houck became a folk-hero; it could not have been otherwise because "public sentiment favored him . . . he was a local man fighting a big corporation."[3] If Jay Gould could be cast as an unscrupulous railway Goliath, Louis Houck could play the role of innocent David before the courts and press by striving to save two small roads. Each road was approximately one hundred miles long, running west and south of Cape Girardeau, Missouri, a river town on the Mississippi almost equi-distant between St. Louis and Memphis.[4] Houck's slingshot ammunition in

23

his fight to save them was endless litigation. This was fair enough, and certainly not a secret weapon unknown to the business community. In 1886 Charles and Henry Adams' dramatic account of the Goulds in their *Chapters of Erie* demonstrated that legal manipulation was the financially rewarding pastime of America's famous "robber barons."[5]

On March 3, 1893, on petition of E. G. Merriam, a Gould lawyer, Eli Klotz was appointed provisional receiver of the first Houck railroad by Judge John G. Wear of the Circuit Court of Stoddard County, Missouri. Of one million dollars of bonds outstanding on this line, Gould interests held some $80,000 of the road's original divisional bonds.[6] Klotz disarmingly stated his case: ". . . all I want is simply for them to pay their honest debts. I have applied for a receiver so that I and the rest of the bondholders can get what is due them."[7] As far as the press was concerned, perhaps he did protest too much by denying that such legal procedure constituted absorption of the small road by the Missouri Pacific, Gould railroad property.[8]

The "panic" year of 1893 was indeed a year of many reverses for Houck's first railroad venture.[9] From a high point set in 1891, passenger earnings had dropped $16,000, and freight earnings, $30,000. Expenses of operation had increased $25,000, making net earnings per mile approximate $17. Washouts necessitated new expenses. Railroad commissioners of Missouri demanded that net earnings be reinvested in the venture in order to improve the road's poor physical condition. Parts of track were reported out of line. In the interest of public safety it was recommended that in certain areas trains not exceed a limit of ten miles per hour, and in other locations, not more than six.

To maintain the fiction that the Goulds desired such "valuable" property was difficult, but Houck persisted in his theme.[10] Possibly he was more correct when he contended that the Goulds wanted to collect their interest ahead of all other bondholders, particularly the Mercantile Trust of New York, trustees for $650,000 of the million dollar indebted-

ness, a company which had been authorized by some of its
stockholders on March 1, 1893, to bring suit in a United
States Circuit Court for foreclosure of the mortgage. Upon
notification of such plan, George Gould, who included in
his many directorships one in the Mercantile Trust, "instructed his attorneys to find a local client to give State
jurisdiction . . . in order to shut out and get ahead of the
Mercantile Trust Company"[11] thereby securing his interest
share of the Cape Girardeau railroad's original divisional
bonds.

Houck was fully aware that receivership was pending.
He simply did not anticipate its occurrence—on March 3,
1893 on petition of a Gould lawyer—without advance notice
to himself. As a quick countermeasure, on March 4, in the
Common Pleas Court of Cape Girardeau, with the trustees
in mortgages of the road acting as defendants, Louis Houck,
in the name of his railroad, asked that a receiver be appointed.[12] Judge Alexander Ross obliged by naming as receiver Louis Houck, president of the road, thereby giving
the road the dubious distinction of having acquired two receivers within forty-eight hours: first, Klotz, provisionally
appointed by a circuit court; second, Houck, appointed by a
city common pleas court.

Unfortunately for Gould interests, Judge Wear, who was
to have rendered the Klotz receivership permanent on March
13, 1893, was absent from the circuit court in the interim of
provisional and final appointment. It was said that he was
"so ill that he went to bed with his boots on."[13] Because of
the large docket of cases still pending, the local bar was
indignant. Fortunately for Houck interests, the Stoddard
County bar proved sufficiently incensed to elect a temporary
judge to transact intervening judicial business: George Houck,
Louis's brother.[14] In the early morning of March 13, Temporary Judge Houck, who was "supposed to have quickly
disposed of 326 cases on the docket for that term,"[15] obligingly
vacated, and annulled the appointment of Eli Klotz at the
request of Louis Houck's attorneys. He then adjourned court
for the term and disappeared into the northern part of the

county. When Judge Wear arrived at a later hour, the dilemma was solved to his satisfaction by expunging orders made by the temporary judge, by qualifying Klotz as receiver by an approval of his bond, and by authorizing him to take physical possession of the property. The regular judge also accepted application for change of venue, transferring the complicated case to Iron County, Missouri. When the Gould legal counsel arrived in Houck's office the following day to secure control of the property, they were met with a restraining injunction forbidding interference with operation of the road or with Houck as its receiver. As last resort, Gould's legal team then made a request for a writ of mandamus from the Missouri Supreme Court to compel Judge Ross of the Cape Girardeau Court of Common Pleas to vacate his appointment of Houck as receiver and surrender the road to Klotz.[16]

The newspapers had a field day. One attempted to explain the mere fact that a road undergoing receivership proceedings was not necessarily in harassed circumstance.[17] Its editor's curious explanation was that generally new railroads must first be managed by receivers whose duties under law were to pay running expenses, maintain roads in good condition, and then reduce bonded indebtedness with any accumulated surpluses. Just because certain lawyers "reside in the backwoods and live off turnip greens," asserted another paper, "is no indication that they are not versed in the law."[18] From the press came the suggestion that recent legal maneuvering constituted an act of desperation by the Missouri Pacific to wreck a local railroad destined to build north to St. Louis and south to Memphis.[19]

In the first round of the case, the Supreme Court of Missouri decided that Judge Wear, the regular judge, had no right or power to set aside Special Judge Houck's ruling after the circuit court had been adjourned for the term. A special judge's powers were considered as absolute as those of a regular judge. In later years, one legal expert thought it strange that the justices were not indignant because the special judge ruled in matters vitally affecting his brother. The specialist assumed that such decision would not have been affirmed in a more enlightened period.[20] Actually one Supreme Court justice was concerned. Thomas A. Sherwood, in his lone dissenting opinion, termed George Houck's action as special judge "as one of the most high-handed and arbitrary character ever witnessed in a court of justice."[21]

Since several personalities involved in the first Supreme Court case were interested parties in later litigation, motivation of these individuals must be explored. Thomas A. Sherwood, lone dissenter in the original judgment, was always opposed to Houck in later cases. Elected to the Supreme Court in 1872, 1882, 1892, he was defeated in 1902. In that year,

> the legal and political influences of the then dominant railroad interests were very active in his support, but these were nullified by innumerable personal and professional animosities developed during a long career because of his aggressive and provocative personality.[22]

Then, too, Sherwood, the justice most concerned about Houck kinships, was brother-in-law of Judge Wear, whom other members of the court decided acted in excess of authority.[23]

Because the Goulds were to turn to Judge John G. Wear's jurisdiction in later receivership cases involving Houck lines, Houck thought that Wear's position needed clarification. He called attention to Wear as former attorney and stock-claim agent for the Missouri Pacific. But more pertinent, Houck claimed, was that the Judge's son, Charles Wear, was under indictment for murder of an employee of the Iron Mountain Railroad, Gould property, and was to be tried in the Dunklin County Circuit Court by a "special" judge who was an attorney for one of the Gould affiliated roads.[24] The implication was, of course, that Wear, in the interests of his son, was completely tied to the Gould interests and subject to their bidding.

The Wear murder case turned out to be as involved as the Houck receiverships, litigation running from 1893 to 1898, the approximate time period of Houck's legal difficulties.[25] Eventually Charles Wear was indicted for murder in the first degree in Butler County, Missouri, for killing Charles Leal. As Charles Wear was the son of the circuit judge of that area, special judges were deemed necessary to conduct the trials. At different times and for varying legal technicalities, several judges including H. C. Riley acted upon the case. Charles Wear was convicted of murder in the second degree and given a thirty-five year sentence in 1895 by Judge Riley. John G. Wear questioned Riley's neutrality because, as circuit judge of Cape Girardeau County, Riley was involved in Houck's receivership cases.[26] As for Houck, Wear stated, his "venom was manifest, and I learned from public and private sources that he was moving everything to embarrass me by interfering in my son's prosecution, for the sole reason that my action in naming a receiver displeased him."[27] Backed by a battery of Gould lawyers, Charles Wear was discharged from imprisonment and acquitted of crime by the Missouri Supreme Court in 1898, despite a conviction under Riley, and previous indictment by grand jury in 1893.[28]

The judge of the Cape Girardeau Court of Common Pleas, Alexander Ross, to whom Houck first turned for jurisdiction, was not related, unlike other principals, to anyone acting in some capacity in the receivership or murder cases. However, he was once treasurer of the Cape Girardeau railroad.[29] In print he had appeared as a man who thought it fitting to protect "local" interests. When there occurred a possibility that larger railroad concerns might include Cape Girardeau on their lines, Ross expostulated in defense of the Houck system: "If we cannot have a whole wheel, let us have a half one, with spokes running south, west, and north, their terminals and headquarters in this city, moved, controlled, influenced and animated by local interest and enterprise."[30]

Houck had won the first round when the Supreme Court upheld Special Judge George Houck's decrees, but the second round went to the Gould forces in 1894. A writ of prohibition against a common pleas court's exercise of authority was obtained from Missouri's highest court.[31] The justices held that a court of common pleas had no power authorizing it to appoint a receiver; that a corporation could not, on its own motion, apply for the appointment of a receiver; that a court of common pleas had no equity jurisdiction in such matters. Louis Houck was thereby ordered to turn the property over to Klotz.

In an impartial judgment, the same legal expert who considered as legally unsound the first Supreme Court case in which Houck won, viewed the second case as injurious to the Cape Girardeau railroad president. Regarding the point of law that a corporation could not, on its own motion, place its property in the hands of a receiver, the lawyer noted that currently

> . . . the corporation gets some big or little secured or unsecured creditor to bring a suit for a receiver in a federal court merely to "conserve" its property and assets, and the corporation comes into court or goes before the judge in chambers and consents to the appointment of a receiver for whom or which it got the plantiff to apply—which is just another way of saying that a corporation asks for the appointment of a receiver. That is now deemed all right. . . .[32]

Houck appealed to the Supreme Court of the United States, charging the state court had violated the 14th amendment.[33] But as the United States Supreme Court recognized no involvement of federal constitutional questions, it dismissed the appeal. Houck's next strategy was to make motion to vacate the appointment of Klotz as receiver in the Iron County Circuit Court to which venue had been directed. The motion was overruled by the circuit court and dismissed by the Supreme Court of Missouri because an appeal could not be carried from circuit court to supreme court on such a matter.[34] There the case rested. Even Houck's ablest attorney, General John W. Noble, advised retreat.[35]

Having failed in these respects, Houck nevertheless opened the third round in 1895 when he instructed Leo Doyle, trustee under the mortgages, to seek independent suit for foreclosure and appointment of a receiver in the circuit court of Cape Girardeau. On January 11, 1895, Judge H. C. Riley designated Houck to be provisional receiver, and in February confirmed the final appointment.[36] It was as if the contest had been renewed. The identical problem arose: two receivers contesting for the control of one road. However, both receivers were appointed by circuit courts in the latest maneuvering. In addition, Houck had been nominated receiver at the instigation of holders of the original divisional mortgages, rather than by his railroad company. Such action assured Houck of proper legal status as made manifest by recent Supreme Court decisions.

An important part of the strategy also occurred in January, 1895, when Houck legal forces obtained from the state legislature a new statute permitting appeal from a circuit court to the Supreme Court on questions concerning the appointment of a receiver.[37] This enabled Houck to lay all questions before Missouri's highest court the final time. Since "the records and legal documents in this remarkable and important suit [were] so voluminous and [contained] such a multiplicity of legal entanglements,"[38] some newspapers hoped this suit would "finally settle the barefaced attempt of the Missouri Pacific to steal the Cape Girardeau road for the paltry sum of $7,500 which is due on bonds. . . ."[39] Houck evidently felt secure, because he calmly laid plans to extend the line toward Fort Smith, taking a trip in that direction while the court considered the complexities of the case.[40]

> By 1896 the court "rendered a just decision" and: redeemed itself from the odium cast upon it by some of the people of the great state of Missouri—to wit: that it belonged body and soul to the big railroad corporations. It has decided that George Gould—big as he is—cannot legally in the grand state of Missouri swallow up one of our citizens.[41]

It held that a receiver could not be appointed for the whole road on petition of a plaintiff who held a small part of divisional bonds on two sections. These two sections totalled only twenty-six miles, whereas the road was over one hundred miles long.[42] Therefore, Eli Klotz, representing Gould interests, was not entitled to management of the line. The court also held that the Cape Girardeau Circuit Court had legally appointed a receiver on petition of trustees representing bondholders of the entire road, and that the Iron County Circuit Court should have refrained from making appointment in cognizance of the above fact. By this judgment Houck won his battle to keep the Goulds from control of his first railroad.

While litigation was under way from 1893-1896 over Cape Girardeau's first railroad, Louis Houck was plunging into his second major railroad enterprise in southeastern Missouri. He had constructed his line approximately one hundred miles south of his home town by 1896 when, for the second time in his railroad career, he was faced with receivership proceedings. To the press the plot remained the same. Houck was the hero; Samuel Fordyce, president of the St. Louis Southwestern (the "Cotton Belt"), Gould railway property, was the villain. The receivership petition was "another move on the part of the Gould crowd to break down Mr. Houck and drive him out of the business of transportation in this portion of the state and intimidate all others from attempting to build any other railroad in this section."[43]

Suit was brought April 13, 1896, in the Dunklin County Circuit Court—presided over by the now familiar Judge John G. Wear. This time A. J. Kerfoot, stockholder, charged mismanagement,[44] as distinct from Eli Klotz, bondholder, who was disturbed by non-payment of interest.[45] As in Wear's conduct of the first case, the receiver, Samuel Fordyce, was appointed without prior notice to the Houck Railroad Company. Louis Houck not only asserted that the appointment was made in guarded manner, but that Fordyce, with "no

notice of his appointment secretly made," simply asked per-
mission of Houck's nephew, L. B. Houck, superintendent of
the road, to run an engine and special train carrying "a
company of friends" to Kennett, Missouri, temporary headquarters of the southern railroad.[46] There, Fordyce claimed
the road. As Louis Houck was absent, his nephew, L. B.
Houck, represented his uncle as capably as had Louis's
brother, George, in the earlier railroad controversy. L. B.
Houck refused possession, and by means of a tie train blocked
the road at Kennett to avoid Fordyce's further occupancy of
the line. Taking the engine, coaches, and cars, Houck's nephew
crossed the rail line to Caruthersville, the Mississippi River
terminus of Houck's road. There, in another county, Pemiscot,
he maneuvered Houck's company into a better position to
ward off Judge Wear's jurisdictional authority.[47]

In reminiscences of T. R. R. Ely of Kennett, Missouri,
attorney for the Houck line, the story was more complete.[48]
Fordyce, Kerfoot, and their attorneys occupied a sleeper
sidetracked at Kennett during the controversies. North of
the sleeper was a freight train heavily loaded with timber.
When Ely was informed of the court order transferring Houck
property to Cotton Belt officials, he persuaded the Dunklin
County sheriff to ignore his orders temporarily. Then Ely

> immediately went to the yards, and, perhaps in an
> unethical way, instructed the conductor of the
> freight train to open the switch just north of the
> sleeper in which the above named officials were
> quartered and gave the freight train the high-ball
> which he accordingly did.

With terrific force the train struck the open switch just north
of the sidetrack on which the sleeper containing Cotton
Belt officials was located. As a result, the sidetrack was
completely dismantled, and the steel of the railroad twisted
like oxbows. Timber from the freight train was hurled in
every direction. Although the sleeper was hopelessly blocked,
Fordyce and his associates emerged from their private car
unharmed.

According to Ely, the Gould crowd was not then in condition to prevent the engine from being cut loose from the wrecked train and removed to the adjoining county. Once Houck forces had escaped the Wear jurisdiction, timbers of the bridge across Little River, dividing line of the two counties, were sawed to render train pursuit impossible. With delightful reticence Louis Houck publicly referred to the use of physical violence just once. In a letter to the *St. Louis Republic*, June 10, 1896, he stated that by forceful methods, Fordyce had come into possession of a part of the property.

As in the battle of the Cape Girardeau railroad, attorneys of the receiver repaired to Louis Houck's office demanding possession of the books and papers of the company. They were over-confident as they entered Houck's headquarters, unsuitably located in the old Baptist Church of the city.[49] The *St. Louis Globe-Democrat* reported Houck's brilliant reception of his adversaries:

> Mr. Houck had no recourse but to obey the mandate of the court, and he directed his secretary to turn the property over, but to take a complete descriptive receipt of each article, one at a time. He had his secretary begin with the way bills and other similar matters, leaving the books to the last. Each way bill was to be elaborately described, even to the minutest particular; and all this painstaking care would have consumed at least three months before Colonel Fordyce could come into possession.[50]

In the meantime Houck secured, first a temporary, and then a permanent writ of prohibition from the Missouri Supreme Court ordering Fordyce to restore the property.[51] Undoubtedly having learned from previous experience with Houck that a state supreme court was not necessarily the last resort of justice in affairs of this kind, the Cotton Belt officials made recourse to a federal court. Unknown to Houck, the federal court nominated Fordyce as the receiver. Reason for the secrecy, maintained Fordyce, a man of growing wisdom, was that the defendants might wreck, destroy, or make away with the property, books, and records of the company.[52] A metropolitan paper groaned:

Take the case of the St. Louis, Kennett and
Southern Railroad. It is 45 miles long and runs from
Caruthersville, Missouri, through Kennett, to Campbell on the Cotton Belt. They have two locomotives
and thirty cars and enough litigation to keep several
attorneys and a number of Deputy United States
Marshals occupied.[53]

Houck was hurt by the implication of his road's un-
importance. "You do not seem to know," came his stinging
reply, "that this is one of the most valuable railroads in the
State, that it has promptly paid its interest for years, and
that in addition it has conferred a great benefit on two southeast counties by giving them a needed railroad outlet and
river competition."[54] Houck's sarcastic conclusion was that
Fordyce, "an effective champion of the Gould interests," was
only too willing to possess the insignificant railroad.

Three weeks after the Missouri Supreme Court had
rendered its decision in favor of Houck, Federal Judge Elmer
B. Adams of St. Louis concurred. Colonel Fordyce conceded
defeat in a manner reminiscent of E. G. Merriam in the first
controversy. Retreating with the ignominious statement that
he had not solicited the receivership which had been tendered
to him, Fordyce remarked that he personally was disinterested in the matter.[55] Several newspapers thought dif-
ferently, and as Houck had now won two complex cases,
citizens of Cape Girardeau, led by the Cape City Band and
Captain Hunze's Light Artillery Company, serenaded Houck
at his country estate.[56] Other towns in Missouri staged cele-
brations. "Now is the time for Houck to run for Congress,"
hinted one paper. Reflecting upon the current excitement, the
editor added, "it is likely he prefers being a railroad magnet
to being a Congressman."[57]

Opponent of Jay and George Gould by proclamation,
Louis Houck derived popular strength and eventual profit
from position of underdog. Accurately gauging public opinion,
he cast himself in the popular role of strategic defender
of local areas dominated by a great railroad overlord. His
success as professional adversary derived in large measure

from his skill in utilizing, on small scale, weapons and tactics of the man he chiefly opposed. Jay Gould was perhaps correct when he assessed Houck's aptitude for law as far better than his competence in railroad construction.[58]

In 1896 it was not demonstrable that Houck's defense of short line railroad construction lacked long-term substance and that his concern for operating efficiency was nominal at best. It was not known, perhaps even to Houck himself, that in five years time railroad properties which had been the subject of so much litigation would be willingly surrendered to larger corporate control. The public was content in 1896 that "perhaps in the course of human events . . . the Missouri Pacific people who have been moving heaven and earth to down Mr. Houck will [have realized] that it is a little risky to meddle with a buzz-saw."[59]

Yet Houck capitulated to stronger railroad interests. He lost his first line by foreclosure at the turn of the century. The southern system, over-capitalized by its purchasers as the St. Louis and Gulf, was considered as possible explanation for the St. Louis-San Francisco railroad debacle of 1913. Between the two world wars, Houck's northern system, through disuse, slowly disappeared from the face of the Missouri railroad map.[60]

NOTES TO CHAPTER II

[1] *St. Louis Republic,* June 7, 1896.

[2] *St. Louis Republic,* June 10, 1896.

[3] *Democrat Argus* (Caruthersville, Missouri), July 14, 1946. (Reminiscences of a business associate of Louis Houck.)

[4] The organizational structure and chronology of building may be found in Appendix D. Financial reports may be found in Appendices A, B, and C.

[5] Charles F. Adams, Jr., and Henry Adams, *Chapters of Erie and Other Essays* (New York, 1886).

[6] Henry Wollman, "The Strange Story of the Cape Girardeau Railroad," *Commercial Law Journal,* June, 1933, p. 1.

[7] *St. Louis Post-Dispatch,* March 11, 1893.

[8] *St. Louis Republic,* March 28, 1894.

[9] *19th Annual Report of Railroad and Warehouse Commissioners of Missouri* (1893), p. 29.

[10] *St. Louis Republic,* March 15, 1893. (Contains Houck's evaluation of his property's value.)

[11] *St. Louis Republic,* March 15, 1893.

[12] Robert G. Ranney, "The City's Railroads," *City Directory of Cape Girardeau for 1906* (Cape Girardeau, Missouri, 1906), p. 202.

[13] *St. Louis Republic,* March 15, 1893.

[14] See *Revised Statutes of Missouri,* 1889, section 3326. Under Missouri laws, when a circuit judge did not show up in court, the members of the bar present, if five were present, elected a special judge who had every power of a regular circuit judge.

[15] Ranney, p. 202.

[16] "The State *ex rel.* Klotz vs. Ross, *et al., Missouri Reports,* CXVIII (November 9, 1893), 23-79.

[17] *Cape Girardeau Democrat,* March 11, 1893.

[18] *Cape Girardeau Democrat,* March 15, 1893.

[19] *Perryville Sun* (Perryville, Missouri), March 25, 1893.

[20] Wollman, p. 4.

[21] *Missouri Reports,* CXVIII, *op. cit.*

[22] Thomas S. Barclay, "Thomas A. Sherwood," *Dictionary of American Biography,* XVII (New York, 1935), 102-103.

[23] Ranney, p. 200.

[24] *St. Louis Republic,* March 15, 1893.

[25] *Jefferson City State Tribune,* June 26, 1898; also see *Cape Girardeau Democrat,* January 25, 1896, and February 1, 1896.

[26] *St. Louis Republic,* June 23, 1895.

[27] *St. Louis Republic,* June 20, 1895.

[28] See "The State vs. Wear," *Missouri Reports,* CXLV (June 25, 1896), 162-230; also "The State *ex rel.* Renfro, Prosecuting Attorney, vs. Wear, Judge, *et al.,*" *Missouri Reports,* CXXIX (July 2, 1895), 619-29.

[29] *Cape Girardeau Democrat,* November 24, 1906.

[30] *Cape Girardeau Democrat,* March 6, 1897.

[31] "State *ex rel.* Merriam, Petitioner, vs. Ross, Judge, *et al., Missouri Reports,* CXXII (June 4, 1894), 435-78.

[32] Wollman, pp. 5-6.

[33] "Missouri *ex rel.* Merriam vs. St. Louis, Cape Girardeau and Fort Smith Railway Company," *United States Reports,* CXXVI (January 22, 1895), 478-85.

[34] "Merriam vs. the St. Louis, Cape Girardeau and Fort Smith Railway, *et al.,* Appellants," *Missouri Reports,* CLVI (January 22, 1895), 445-8.

[35] Noble was formerly the Secretary of the Interior in the Benjamin Harrison administration and the man under whom Houck had worked when he was assistant district attorney in St. Louis in 1869. Wollman, p. 3.

[36] "Merriam vs. St. Louis, Cape Girardeau and Fort Smith Railway Company," *Missouri Reports,* CXXXVI (December 1, 1896), 145-69.

[37] *Journal of Senate of 38th General Assembly of Missouri* (1895), pp. 437 and 853; *Journal of the House of Representatives* (1895), p. 1036; *Laws of Missouri, 38th General Assembly* (1895), p. 91; *Jefferson City Daily Tribune,* April 12, 1895.

[38] *Jefferson City Daily Tribune,* June 24, 1896.

[39] *Cape Girardeau Democrat,* May 4, 1895.

[40] *17th Annual Report of the Railroad and Warehouse Commissioners of Missouri* (1891), p. 25.

[41] *Cape Girardeau Democrat,* June 22, 1896. Also see *St. Louis Republic,* June 24, 1896.

[42] *Missouri Reports,* CXXXVI, *op. cit.* Also see "State *ex rel.* Merriam vs. Ross *et al.*" *Missouri Reports,* CXXXVI (December 1, 1896), 259-75.

[43] *Cape Girardeau Democrat,* April 18, 1896.

[44] The charge of mismanagement centered on the substitution of Houck's nephew for Kerfoot as an official on the line, without sufficient notice or compensation to Kerfoot.

[45] *Cape Girardeau Democrat,* April 18, 1896.

[46] *St. Louis Republic,* June 10, 1896.

[47] *Dunklin Democrat* (Kennett, Missouri), April 19, 1938 (anniversary edition).

[48] Account from unidentified newspaper located in Southeast Missouri State College Kent Library, Cape Girardeau, Missouri.

[49] *Democrat Argus* (Caruthersville, Missouri), July 12, 1946.

[50] *St. Louis Globe-Democrat,* June 16, 1896.

[51] "St. Louis, Kennett and Southern Railroad Company *et al. vs.* Wear, Judge, *et al.*," *Missouri Reports,* CXXXV (June 30, 1896), 230-69.

[52] *St. Louis Republic,* June 7, 1896.

[53] *Ibid.*

[54] *St. Louis Republic,* June 10, 1896.

[55] *St. Louis Republic,* June 24, 1896.

[56] *Cape Girardeau Democrat,* June 27, 1896.

[57] *Cairo Daily Argus,* reprinted in *Cape Girardeau Democrat,* July 11, 1896.

[58] *Enterprise Courier* (Charleston, Missouri), February 26, 1925 (Reminiscences of a business associate of Louis Houck).

[59] *Cape Girardeau Democrat,* July 18, 1896.

[60] See *Cape Girardeau Democrat,* January 21, 1899, and Wollman, p. 14, as to collapse of Houck's first system; *Cape Girardeau Democrat,* May 3, 1902, and William Z. Ripley, *Railroads, Finance and Organization* (New York, 1915), p. 41, for sale of the second railroad network.

CHAPTER III

SHORT-LINE RAILROADS, 1880-1910: STUDY IN INCENTIVES

"There is a man in Missouri and that man in Missouri is not to be turned not even by Wall Street capitalists and lawyers."—*Cape Girardeau Democrat*, June 28, 1902.

T HERE WAS considerable justification for the quip that Louis Houck "had a penchant for gathering rails—some old, some new, not very heavy—and making a railroad out of them."[1] In truth, a collection of reports from Missouri railroad and warehouse commissioners on Houck's three transportation systems, which extended some five hundred miles west, south, and north from Cape Girardeau, Missouri, seemed to question whether railroad building had actually been effected.[2] In 1891, commissioners "fully aware of the natural obstacles with which the management of this line [Houck's first railway system] have had to contend on account of the low, swampy country it traverses and the frequency of overflow of the track,"[3] scored sixty out of ninety-five miles as laid with shattered, splintered, twisted, old, worn-out rails; trestles and culverts in shaky condition; and the line badly in need of adequate ditching. Intervals of years between adverse reports resulted not in improvements, but only in continuing deterioration. By 1898, complaints regarding condition of this road and its operation were not only frequent, proclaimed the inspectors, but also well-founded. An inspection disclosed the right-of-way almost entirely unfenced, not over four miles of track ballasted, and all cuts still in need of necessary ditching. A very large proportion of cross-ties were unfit for the purposes intended, and

> in many places from two to five ties consecutively were found broken or completely rotten, intervals

38

of from two to nine feet occurring without any support for the rail except the ground. In many places
the rail is not spiked to the ties and is from one
to two inches clear of them, the consequences being
bad low joints, bent and warped rails, and the track
utterly out of line and surface. Derailments at these
points are frequent, and that lives are not lost or
persons injured thereby, is due more to luck than
management.[4]

Commissioners estimated fifty per cent of the bridges,
trestles, and cattleguards unfit for service. One particularly
harrowing inspection incident was recorded:

Whilst we were at a point about two miles east of a
tunnel, a local freight train carrying passengers,
the train consisting of about 18 cars, and with the
locomotive in the centre of the train, passed us at
a speed of not less than 35 miles per hour. We are
free to say that in all our railroad experiences of
many years, we never witnessed a more reckless dis-
regard of reasonable precautions than was shown in
this instance.[5]

Shortly before the system west of Cape Girardeau passed
from Houck's control, state commissioners bluntly warned
that "to continue its operation in its present condition and
in the manner witnessed by us, is at the great risk of life,
person and property."[6]

In the capacity of roving correspondent Louis Houck
had predicted in 1869 that the second system running south
of Cape Girardeau would require little construction effort.
He had estimated that "it will cost less to build a railroad
through this county [Dunklin] than through any county in
the South East. All that is necessary . . . is put down the ties
and nail the rails upon them."[7]

Though there were no official reports of inspection of
any of Houck's southernmost lines constructed in the years
1891 to 1902, local reminiscences affirmed that Houck had
built cheaply in accordance with his original appraisal. One
writer recalled that along the southern route was a cyprus
stump so big it defied implements of the construction crew.

The problem was resolved by building around the tree; workmen "described a crescent as picturesque as a new moon in the western sky."[8] In many places piling was driven and cross ties laid thereon, "but a securer foundation was more quickly made by sawing off the tupelos at the water's edge so that the progress of the work might not be delayed." As Houck did not build all of his second system, the condition of his purchased property revealed at least that he had conformed to a pattern of inadequate construction set by other southeast Missouri railway architects. An account of one of his purchased sections read: ". . . the original road was not built to any grade . . . within a few miles of Kennett the tracks were actually curved to go around stumps and large trees."[9] In winter months the engine could not manufacture enough steam to pull the train over steep grades, causing irregular service to become a regular feature. The complete inadequacy of the building methods used on a portion of Houck's purchase was described as follows:

> . . . the track was laid, without any railroad dump
> or prepared track bed, on poles that were cut along
> the railroad right-of-way . . . sand was brought in by
> train, moved over the track and dumped. The track
> and poles were jacked up, permitting the sand to
> infiltrate between and under the ties. The sand was
> stamped in place and the poles from time to time
> were replaced with cross ties.[10]

Houck's third system north of Cape Girardeau fared no better in official railway publications. In 1907 commissioners refused to particularize on the condition of the road because it was badly out of repair its entire length.[11] Nevertheless, in fulfillment of their public obligations, the inspectors reported the road's rails badly warped, as well as broken and patched, and some without any adequate support. Cuts, without exception, were in deplorable condition, causing even the observation car to become stalled because of muddy tracks. Two years later commissioners discovered that ties remained in poor condition. Since they were in a state of rapid decay, ties "should be speedily removed and new ones put in their places."[12] Because of the line's inadequate fencing, one farmer sued Houck for the cost of sixty bushels of wheat destroyed by roaming cattle.[13] Other claims for damages because of personal injuries suffered on the Houck trains were forthcoming.[14] Not only were adverse assessments of the third system comparable to reports on the other two networks, but also there was similarity in operation. One paper calmly narrated:

> The Chester and Perryville railroad came near losing one of their engines last week. The engine shoved several cars of wheat out on the incline opposite Chester and when it started back it jumped the track. Had the engine moved a few inches farther it would have toppled into the river.[15]

Poor construction was explained not only by the obvious fact that it was inexpensive, but also by the lack of skilled labor in the area. In articles published in the *Missouri Republican* in the years 1869-1870, Houck had expressed displeasure with the scarcity of labor and the unreliability of the southeastern Missouri Negro. In the November 2, 1869, issue he castigated the "American citizen of African descent who prefers coon hunting in the Little River swamp to other forms of endeavor." Yet in the period of actual construction, Houck obviously turned to Negro employment and was dissuaded from it only because of the sentiments of southerners in the bootheel section of the state. The *Cape Girardeau Democrat* broadcast that "the old moss backs of Dunklin County will not allow negroes to work on the railroad."[16] When thirty-five Negro laborers were assigned to washout repairs on the Kennett and Caruthersville railroad, the paper reported that "the Dunklin County moss backs drove them off." Negroes were not used in 1913, according to one paper, because they had increased their wage demands to $2.50 per day.[17] Work stoppages were once explained by the Greek, Bulgarian and Servian War. Labor crews employed on the Houck lines had been summoned home for military service.

Houck, the lawyer-journalist, freely admitted that he lacked rudimentary mechanical knowledge. Yet, on occasion, the accidental railroad director found himself "bolting rails, carrying spikes, and angle plates, and spreading and bossing the spreading of ties—in fact doing everything that I could do."[18] He complained that when he resorted to foreign construction crews, they performed their services inadequately.[19]

Jerry type construction may have been due, in part, to the character of the countryside the railroads traversed. At the time Houck commenced his building "the alluvial valley of southeast Missouri was a vast waste of swamp land. Farming was engaged in only to the extent of supplying the needs of the family table."[20] In an estimate of the first system, it was stated that roadbeds were greatly damaged by muskrats and beavers honeycombing the lines with holes.[21] In a description of lands traversed by the second system, it was stated that "The swamp was so dense with timber growth that it was very easy for a person to become totally lost, especially someone not familiar with direction in the timbered country."[22] In fact, a hunter separated from his companions wandered for two days before discovering an outlet in the area.

Yet for all the problems involving technological ignorance, labor scarcity, and physiography of southeast Missouri, newspapers inferred that there was another and brighter side to short-line railroad construction in such a region. According to local estimates, Houck lines were encompassing an expanse wealthy in natural resources. Therefore, Houck could expect profitable tonnage as soon as the unexploited area became accessible to the outside world. Later eulogies of the short-line railroad builder claimed that when Louis Houck left St. Louis in 1869 for permanent residence in southeast Missouri, "there were millions of acres of land in the southeast part of the state which [were] without other outlet for their products than the Mississippi River."[23] It was estimated that 30,000 acres of timber had been cleared in Pemiscot County by 1897, but that probably 225,000 acres of good merchantable timber remained.[24] In reference to Houck's Kennett line, one paper advertised that "this road runs through a very finely timbered country and one of the best cotton-producing districts in the state."[25] Another

paper calculated that the extension to Caruthersville would
be a paying one

> for the simple reason that the entire line is built
> through a section of the country, the soil of which
> is as fertile as the far famed valley of the Nile,
> and the portion that is in cultivation yields immense
> crops of corn, cotton, potatoes, and in fact every-
> thing the farmer chooses to grow; while the unim-
> proved land is covered with an enormous growth of
> the most valuable timber, which will be converted
> into lumber by a number of fine saw mills soon to
> be erected along the line of this road.[26]

Houck lines, commented one editor,

> traverse probably the richest sections of Missouri
> and Northeast Arkansas. The alluvial soil south of
> Cape Girardeau in the St. Francis Basin covers
> between 4,000 and 5,000 square miles, and will sup-
> ply a good timber, as well as a good agricultural
> traffic.[27]

Houck's northern lines would be an advantage to Missouri
towns; they would obtain "cheaper and quicker freight
facilities and at the same time open up the northern part
of the country which is rich in farming products and whose
earth covers untold mineral wealth."[28]

Houck catered primarily to extractive industrial interests
of the state during his period of ownership and control. The
railway west of Cape Girardeau serviced the William Brown
stave factory and the T. J. Moss railroad tie company. With
the introduction of Brown as a Houck customer, Houck's
first enterprise appeared prosperous to speculators. On March
6, 1882, the *Missouri Republican* heralded "the business boom
and prosperity, the tidal wave of life and enterprise" which
Brown and Moss had brought to Cape Girardeau. Editorially,
the *Cape Girardeau Democrat* considered T. J. Moss, with the
exception of Louis Houck, the greatest benefactor to southeast
Missouri.[29] Moss, a multimillionaire, was then the largest
railroad tie contractor in the United States.

On the second system south of Cape Girardeau were
located Gideon and Anderson, sawmill promoters; the

Himmelberger-Luce timber interests; C. A. Boynton, owner
of sawmills and planing mills; and the Deering lumber interests. Boynton owned 60,000 acres of land in Missouri and
Arkansas.[30] The town of Deering was established in 1902
as the center of the lumber industry of the International
Harvester Company [McCormick and Deering] of Indiana-
polis, Indiana.[31] At the time of the establishment of the
Gideon-Anderson Lumber Company "there was only a little
clearing in the all but impassable swamp and the country
around was virgin forest. . . . Their mill had a capacity of
10,000 feet per day. . . ."[32] Himmelberger and Harrison of
the Luce Land and Lumber Company controlled 200,000
acres of land in southeast Missouri and operated the biggest
hardwood sawmill in the United States.[33]

The Byrd milling interests at Jackson, Missouri, were
located on the northern network.[34] However, there was dis-
turbing evidence that Houck's third line was projected
through a tract of land not quite as ripe for quick extraction
of wealth as was the area serviced by the southern railways.
One newspaper editor admonished the citizens along the
more settled agrarian route:

> Farmers, wake up to the demands of the new day.
> Mr. Houck has given you a railroad to your doors
> and linked you to the wealthy markets of the North
> and East, markets that will take every berry, every
> pound of butter, every chicken, turkey, goose, and
> dozen of eggs you can produce. Level up those
> neglected spots and set them to orchard, grass, and
> clover, or cow peas, then plant them to small fruits,
> anything, only level them and plow them.[35]

Yet another journal hinted that the northern line had been
built in the interests of extractive industry.[36] One extension
of the line was reported as constructed for the purpose of
supplying southern Illinois coal to smelters and other large
industries in the lead belt of Missouri.

Houck took advantage of the competition of towns for
positions on railroad outlets in periods when "veritable crazes
of promotion and speculation, unequalled before or since in

our railroad history"[37] were culminating. West Plains, a town on the Kansas City, Fort Scott and Memphis line, believed that it would procure in the way of an additional outlet a Houck extension ". . . if any efforts are made in that direction . . . if our people have not lost all their enterprise and town pride."[38] One account states that in November, 1882, "Louis Houck drove down to Commerce [Missouri] in his buggy, from Cape Girardeau, and in the old courthouse there, organized a class in primitive railroad building."[39] There follows, in this account, a list of those who "matriculated" in such a course and amounts of their generous subscription fees. A Jackson, Missouri, newspaper stated that since Houck had not built roads without the encouragement and assistance of local people, "it is not supposed that he will do more for us than he ought to do and has done for other sections."[40] Enthusiastic over the possibility of a Houck line coming into its city, a Perryville, Missouri paper commented that "it is the duty of every progressive citizen to give it all the encouragement possible."[41] The *Farmington Times* succumbed to the desire for a Houck extension when it editorialized:

> Let us see what will be the consequences if the Saline Valley Railroad does not come to Farmington. Just now it is operating to Coffman, and from there gets fifty or sixty cars of wheat that used to be hauled in here by wagon, but which is now sold to the Cape County Milling Company down there. Farmers with their wives and families who used to come up and trade all through the summer are hardly ever seen any more. Wire, cement, fertilizer, and other things that they used to buy here they now get at Coffman. About the only thing they have not got that they need is a bank, and we hear it won't be long before they have that.[42]

Available though widely scattered evidence indicates that Houck's lines were projected for the following considerations: expectation of land subsidies (nullified by state and national regulatory action),[43] transportation of products of large landowners and lumber companies, and local subsidization by citizens of southeast Missouri towns anxious for location on some rail line. Because Houck lines often made connection with the larger Gould railway systems in southeast Missouri, Gould may have purchased these lines for the protection of his own monopoly as well as for litigious relief. As it was Gould's technique either to buy off or destroy competition,[44] Houck's short-line construction seemed as reasonable as it was daring. Adverse reports of the Missouri railway commission had certainly suggested that although solid construction would seem to be a vital factor in fulfilling Cape Girardeau's ambition to become her own "gateway to the West," Houck's railroad building was not designed to be of a permanent nature. That the Houck roads would disappear either because of physical deterioration, or because they would pass on to other concerns more financially capable of reconstruction was the implied, if unwritten, theme of the state railroad inspectors. As already noted, the western and southern systems were eventually surrendered to larger corporate control, and the northern system simply faded in time from the Missouri railroad map.[45]

Houck's harassment of the Gould properties took many forms. Such vexation might not be profitable, but it proved popular with southeast Missourians; there was a tendency to interpret every Houck annoyance of the Gould interests as a moral victory. Apparently no one realized that Houck was making capital of his own economic vulnerability, and was boldly employing the very tactics for which the public was condemning his formidable adversary. One fairly innocent form of harassment, of possible public benefit, was securing for Houck lines dissatisfied business concerns located on Gould lines. T. J. Moss, an important Houck customer, was disgruntled with Gould, who, upon assumption of the management of the Union Pacific, had cancelled a previous large order of railroad ties originally contracted by Charles Francis Adams.[46] William Brown was another dissatisfied former customer of Gould. The Byrd milling interests and the Himmelberger lumber concern, by having locations on both Gould and Houck lines, could undoubtedly play both ends against the middle in securing favorable freight rates.[47]

Small incidents of pestering undoubtedly had their cumulative effect upon both parties. When Gould interests purportedly sold Houck inferior rails, Houck retaliated with non-payment as well as suit. Gould journeyed to Charleston, Missouri, to hear the short-line railroad director, acting as his own lawyer, conduct the case.[48] Not only did Gould remain one week aboard his special train of five cars because he was entranced by the trial, he was reported to have brought the litigation to a dramatic conclusion with the declaration: "Let him have his damn rails for nothing if he'll drop proceedings against my road."[49] According to the same reporter, Houck had another brush with the Goulds when he attempted to cross their tracks at Morley, Missouri, with his Missouri and Arkansas railroad.[50] Gould operators, in order to block his crossing, constructed a switch and filled it with cars. Houck, according to the reminiscences, conveyed the right-of-way which crossed the Gould railroad to the town board of Morley for a city thoroughfare, with the proviso that he might run his tracks through the street. This in turn enabled the town authorities to order removal of the Gould cars out of the switch because a public passageway was obstructed.

Naturally the Gould interests could retaliate. The *Cape Girardeau Democrat* reported one of Houck's northern railway companies responsible for condemnation of a twenty-four acre tract of land belonging to a Gould line.[51] The Cape Bell Telephone Company, through Houck's intercession, procured a right-of-way for its long distance telephone poles. In addition, Houck's company was partially utilizing the condemned property for depot and yard purposes. When the telephone crew proceeded to erect its poles, a Gould force of twenty-five men threw the poles over the fence. When the telephone men began digging other holes, the Gould crew filled the holes with dirt. Who was the final victor in the fracas was never reported.

More significant than these minor skirmishes was Houck's inability to secure adequate "through" connections for his customers. Gould held the better connections within

the large cities and outside the state. Nevertheless, Houck
dared to strike back, however wide his swing might have
been. Rather than surrender his outgoing railroad freight
to Gould, he organized steamboat lines which carried his
tonnage from Cape Girardeau via the Mississippi River to
St. Louis and points in Illinois.[52] He backed the promotion
of lines in the neighboring state of Illinois.[53] All of this
enabled him to testify: "I am a through line to St. Louis;
that through line is the Anchor Line and my road."[54] Four
years later he was boasting that ". . . by means of a steamboat, a river route for the transportation of lumber and
cattle, goods and merchandise to and from the city of St.
Louis," the productions of the southeastern portion of the
state were assured of an unbroken short eastern outlet. But
it was doubtful that potential customers were completely
convinced. Comparison of returns of the paralleled and intertwined roads indicated that in southeast Missouri, Gould's
larger earnings easily made him victor financially over
Houck.[55]

When the railroad director of one of Gould's affiliated
lines, Colonel S. W. Fordyce of the St. Louis Southwestern,
sought passage for his trains over one of Houck's lines into
Cape Girardeau, Missouri, the motivation of profits via
litigious harassment seemed conspicuous.[56] The St. Louis
Southwestern, located in southeast Missouri, had working
arrangements with Gould's Iron Mountain Railroad, which
gave it an outlet to St. Louis.[57] Cape Girardeau entry was
evidently sought, because by crossing the Mississippi River
at that point, the St. Louis Southwestern could be provided
with Chicago outlets via the Wabash system or via small
lines being purchased by the Chicago and Eastern Railroad
and the Illinois Central Railroad.[58]

The two railroad directors were unable to conclude an
agreement, Colonel Fordyce stating that Houck, by throwing
every conceivable obstacle in his way, would not let him
enter.[59] Fordyce's defiance as well as independence of Houck
was demonstrated by his construction of a fifteen mile line

from a point on his railroad to Gray's Point, a few miles south of Cape Girardeau.[60] The *St. Louis Republic* had warned that Fordyce's plans would "either do a great deal for the upbuilding of the present town of Cape Girardeau, or affect that place adversely, it depending entirely where the terminals are placed."[61] A Cape Girardeau paper retaliated with the prediction, "The youngest citizen will not live long enough to see that road built to Gray's Point."[62] The warning of the St. Louis journal was well-advised; the prediction of the Cape newspaper was wrong. It later conceded "that thousands of dollars of trade that had been coming to this town for the last 25 years" had been lost.[63] Lines in Illinois began to converge opposite Gray's Point, enabling Fordyce to effect the necessary freight exchanges.[64]

Crucial aspect of the rivalry came, however, over location of a railroad bridge at either Cape Girardeau or Gray's Point.[65] The *Cape Girardeau Democrat* urged the state politicians to convince the national congress that the bridge ought not be "at Gray's Point, Goose Neck, or some other place 5 or 6 miles away."[66] But Representative George W. Smith of Illinois argued cogently for the location of the bridge at Gray's Point because the structure would be used by big and reliable corporations (the Missouri Pacific, the Illinois Central, and the St. Louis Southwestern) which would be relieved of constructing unnecessary mileage into Cape Girardeau.[67] The only road to be benefited by the Cape location, declared Smith, was a Houck line "which ended at Cape Girardeau and began some place in the woods of Missouri."[68] Congress approved Gray's Point as the Missouri terminal of the proposed Southern Illinois and Missouri bridge.[69]

Houck was unwilling to concede defeat. On the day of its incorporation, a new Houck railroad company, the Cape Girardeau and Thebes Bridge Terminal, purchased the "Stone Farm" property, and thus secured complete control of all the land north, south, and west of the Missouri terminal of the projected bridge.[70] This was accomplished a few hours prior to the Illinois bridge company's application for condemnation of the Stone property in their own interest.[71]

The inevitable, tortuous litigation ensued.[72] When a Dunklin County, Missouri circuit judge dismissed the bridge company's request on the grounds that a business organization incorporated by another state had no power to condemn lands in Missouri, the *Cape Girardeau Democrat* was jubilant. It assured its readers that although Houck's company was now secure in all approaches to the bridge, Houck would put in tracks for the accommodation of all railroads desiring to utilize the bridge, but "of course the railroads will have to pay something for the use of these tracks."[73]

The *St. Louis Republic*, on May 23, 1902, perhaps best stated what the price would be. Louis Houck's terminal company wanted a one-sixth proprietary interest in the bridge. As the matter now stood, commented the paper, the Illinois Central, the Chicago and Eastern Illinois, the Iron Mountain, the Missouri Pacific, and the St. Louis Southwestern each owned a one-fifth interest in the property. If Houck was allowed his one-sixth interest, one-half the bridge would be owned by Gould interests (the Iron Mountain, the St. Louis Southwestern, and the Missouri Pacific) and the other half by outside parties. "It is evident," concluded the paper, "that something of no small value is involved in this struggle."

The Cape papers contemplated the catastrophe facing the Goulds:

> The fight between the Thebes Bridge Company and the Thebes Bridge Terminal Railroad Company is now on and all kinds of injunctions and writs of prohibitions are being issued. The Bridge Company went at the little railroad company laughing till they discovered that Louis Houck was in the background, then their smiles changed to frowns. When the attorneys for the bridge spied Louis Houck sitting on the hill top near the west end of the proposed bridge, gazing down toward the river with the monarch of all he surveyed look upon his face, they realized they were up against it good and strong, and now they do not know what to do or where to go.[74]

Several months later, as the case wended its way to the Supreme Court, the paper was still entertaining its readers with such accounts as:

There is something wrong down at Thebes and Gray's Point. It may be that the projectors of the bridge have struck shallow water, but we are inclined to believe that they have been butting their heads up against a man in Missouri and thereby found it was shallow heads they had struck on the bridge projection's shoulders and not shallow water.[75]

Jubilant reporting was premature. The Supreme Court of Missouri decided that the bridge company had the right to condemn lands;[76] on certain technicalities the Supreme Court of the United States ruled against the Houck interests;[77] and on still other occasions the Supreme Court of Missouri denied all of Houck's legal contentions.[78] Louis Houck had definitely lost the battle of the bridge in all major court decisions. The Cape Girardeau and Thebes Bridge Company, failing in its original purpose, simply became a part of Houck's northern system when its line was extended into Cape Girardeau to connect with other Houck properties.[79]

Houck had demonstrated that legal harassments by a small-line railroad builder were often motivated by economic considerations. A local paper characterized Louis Houck not only as a "pusher" but as "a practical and successful railroad builder and the way that he is going at this enterprise shows that he means business."[80]

However, in final analysis, all Houck railroads passed from control of the indefatigable builder. Legal harassment had not always produced profits. By foreclosure in 1899, the western system passed to larger corporate control; by lucrative sale in 1902, the southern system was reorganized into the St. Louis-San Francisco system. The northern network, never a paying proposition, attracted neither passengers nor purchasers. Nevertheless, Louis Houck had procured one hit in three strikes. Complex litigation, however colorful, had not produced victory. Transportation outlets for the extractive industries of heavily timbered southeast Missouri, the essence of his southern system, was the real substance of Louis Houck's railroad career.

Notes to Chapter III

[1] *Southeast Missourian,* Cape Girardeau, Missouri, June 28, 1933.

[2] The first system of Cape Girardeau was approximately 100 miles long and was constructed in the years 1880 to 1890. The second system, south of the city, was some 250 miles long, constructed in the years 1891-1898. North of Cape Girardeau was the third system, built in the years 1895 to 1913. See *Reports of Railroad and Warehouse Commissioners of Missouri* and *Poor's Manual of Railroads* for dates indicated above.

[3] *17th Annual Report of Railroad and Warehouse Commissioners of Missouri* (1891), p. 280.

[4] *23rd Annual Report of Railroad and Warehouse Commissioners of Missouri* (1898), p. 38.

[5] *Ibid.,* p. 40.

[6] *Ibid.,* p. 41.

[7] *Missouri Republican* (St. Louis, Missouri), September 17, 1869.

[8] *Southeast Missourian* (Cape Girardeau, Missouri), March 21, 1934.

[9] *The Kennett Clipper* (Kennett, Missouri), [n.d.], reprinted in *The Dunklin Democrat* (Kennett, Missouri), April 19, 1938.

[10] Hal H. McHaney, "The History of the McHaney Family in Dunklin County, Missouri," *Dunklin County Historical Society* (May 24, 1948), pp. 324-5.

[11] *33rd Annual Report of Railroad and Warehouse Commissioners of Missouri* (1908), p. 127.

[12] *35th Annual Report of Railroad and Warehouse Commissioners of Missouri* (1910), pp. 80-81.

[13] *Daily Republican* (Cape Girardeau, Missouri), January 8, 1909.

[14] *Daily Republican* (Cape Girardeau, Missouri), August 30, 1912.

[15] *The Chester Herald,* reprinted in *The Perry County Republican,* July 27, 1905.

[16] *Cape Girardeau Democrat,* May 13, 1897.

[17] *Weekly Republican* (Cape Girardeau, Missouri), June 6, 1913.

[18] Louis Houck, "Railroad Work" [manuscript, Cape Girardeau, Missouri, n.d.].

[19] *Ibid.*

[20] *St. Louis Post-Dispatch,* June 1, 1929.

[21] Robert G. Ranney, "The City's Railroads," *City Directory of Cape Girardeau, Missouri for 1906*, p. 200.

[22] McHaney, pp. 326-327.

[23] *Missouri Historical Review*, XIX (1925), 475.

[24] *Commercial Appeal* (Memphis, Tennessee), July 16, 1950.

[25] *Cape Girardeau Democrat*, July 18, 1891.

[26] *Cape Girardeau Democrat*, January 5, 1895.

[27] *St. Louis Republic*, November 14, 1902. Also see Sidney Douglass, *History of Southeast Missouri* (Chicago, 1912), p. 370 ff., for description of economic interests of towns along route of Houck's lines.

[28] *Cape Girardeau Democrat*, December 1, 1900.

[29] *Cape Girardeau Democrat*, August 12, 1893.

[30] *Cape Girardeau Democrat*, September 8, 1900.

[31] Mayme Lucille Hamlet, "Place Names of Six Southeast Missouri Counties of Missouri" (unpublished Master's thesis, University of Missouri, Columbia, Missouri, 1938), p. 53.

[32] Douglass, p. 1251.

[33] *Cape Girardeau Democrat*, September 8, 1900.

[34] *St. Louis Post-Dispatch*, January 11, 1914.

[35] *Cape Girardeau Democrat*, December 24, 1904.

[36] *Farmington Times* (Farmington, Missouri), June 22, 1911. Also see *St. Louis Republic*, October 21, 1911.

[37] William Z. Ripley, *Railroads, Rates and Regulation* (New York, 1915), p. 27.

[38] *West Plains Gazette*, reprinted in *Cape Girardeau Democrat*, March 21, 1891.

[39] *Southeast Missourian* (Cape Girardeau, Missouri), March 21, 1934.

[40] *Jackson Cash Book*, reprinted in *Cape Girardeau Democrat*, December 22, 1900.

[41] *Perry County Republican* (Perryville, Missouri), January 23, 1902.

[42] *Farmington Times*, May 19, 1911.

[43] John Eddy Franklin memoirs, *The Democrat Argus* (Caruthersville, Missouri), June 15, 1946 to August 2, 1946; also *Missouri Reports*, CII (October, 1890), 45-46.

44 Robert E. Reigel, "The Missouri Pacific, 1879-1900," *Missouri Historical Review*, XVIII (1924), 173-196.

45 *Cape Girardeau Democrat*, April 12 and September 6, 1902; *St. Louis Post-Dispatch*, January 11, 1914; *51st Report on the Statistics of Railways in the United States* (1937), p. 247; Henry Wollman, *Commercial Law Journal* (June, 1933), p. 14.

46 *Cape Girardeau Democrat*, August 12, 1893.

47 "Morley and Morehouse Railroad Company, *et al.*, vs. John Himmelberger, *et al.*," *Missouri Reports*, CCXLVII (Columbia, Missouri, December 24, 1912), 179-97; *Weekly Republican* (Cape Girardeau, Missouri), January 16, 1914.

48 *Enterprise Courier* (Charleston, Missouri), February 26, 1925.

49 *St. Louis Post-Dispatch*, March 1, 1925.

50 *Enterprise Courier* (Charleston, Missouri), February 26, 1925.

51 *Cape Girardeau Democrat*, September 5, 1903.

52 *Democrat Argus* (Caruthersville, Missouri), July 12, 1946.

53 *19th Annual Report of Railroad and Warehouse Commissioners of Illinois* (1889), pp. 114-115.

54 *Statements and Testimony of Railroad Managers,* 34th General Assembly of Missouri (Jefferson City, Missouri, 1887), p. 352.

55 *17th Annual Report of Railroad and Warehouse Commissioners of Missouri* (1891), p. 121.

56 *Cape Girardeau Democrat*, September 28, 1895.

57 *St. Louis Republic*, June 13, 1896.

58 *St. Louis Republic*, July 31, 1896; *Poor's Manual of Railroads* (1898), p. 207.

59 *Cape Girardeau Democrat*, October 29, 1898; also see *22nd Annual Report of Railroad and Warehouse Commissioners of Missouri,* (1897), pp. 274-83, for description of enmities between the two systems.

60 *Poor's Manual of Railroads* (1899), p. 593.

61 *St. Louis Republic*, June 13, 1896.

62 *Cape Girardeau Democrat*, October 29, 1898.

63 *Cape Girardeau Democrat*, January 21, 1899.

64 *Poor's Manual of Railroads* (1899), pp. 339, 593; *24th Annual Report of Railroad and Warehouse Commissioners of Missouri* (1899), p. 12.

65 *Cape Girardeau Democrat*, April 21, 1900.

66 *Cape Girardeau Democrat,* May 5, 1900.

67 See *30th Annual Report of Railroad and Warehouse Commissioners of Missouri* (1905), for interests supporting the Southern Illinois and Missouri Bridge Company.

68 *Cape Girardeau Democrat,* December 22, 1900.

69 *United States Statutes at Large,* 1899-1901, Ch. 181, p. 741. Also see *Congressional Record,* 56th Cong. 2nd sess., pp. 1183, 1238-9, 1251, 1316, 1644.

70 *27th Annual Report of Railroad and Warehouse Commissioners of Missouri* (1902), pp. 16-17; *Cape Girardeau Democrat,* April 26, 1902.

71 *Missouri Reports,* CCXV (1908), p. 286.

72 *Cape Girardeau Democrat,* May 17, 1902; *St. Louis Republic,* May 4, 1902.

73 *Cape Girardeau Democrat,* May 24, 1902.

74 *Cape Girardeau Democrat,* May 31, 1902.

75 *Cape Girardeau Democrat,* June 28, 1902.

76 "Southern Illinois and Missouri Bridge Company, Appellant, vs. Stone, *et al.,*" *Missouri Reports,* CLXXIV (Columbia, Missouri, April 1, 1903), pp. 1-53.

77 "Stone vs. Southern Illinois and Missouri Bridge Company," *United States Reports,* CCVI (1907), pp. 267-75.

78 "Southern Illinois and Missouri Bridge Company vs. Stone *et al.,* Appellants," *Missouri Reports,* CXCIV (1906), pp. 175-178; "Cape Girardeau and Thebes Bridge Terminal Railroad Company vs. Southern Illinois and Missouri Bridge Company," *Missouri Reports,* CCXV (1908), pp. 286-98.

79 *28th Annual Report of Railroad and Warehouse Commissioners of Missouri* (1903), p. 344.

80 *Farmington Times,* reprinted in *Cape Girardeau Democrat,* March 4, 1893.

CHAPTER IV

OUT OF HISTORICAL STEP: TOLL ROADS AND RECLAMATION

"It is the intensive cultivist against the owner of large tracts who believes that no news is good news, the apostle of radical improvements against the man who desires to let well enough alone."—*St. Louis Republic*, July 29, 1911.

So MANY Missouri papers and periodicals would not have titled Louis Houck an empire builder and father of his section if editors had believed that while engaged in his individual enterprises, Houck had not at the same time been promoting the prosperity of Cape Girardeau in particular, and southeast Missouri in general.[1] Five hundred miles of railroads might have earned Houck his epithets from transportation enthusiasts, but his other Missouri interests helped to establish his titles.[2]

However, there were critics. To the *St. Louis Republic* the heavily propertied Houck was frequently found on the side of individual interests versus the larger interests of the state.[3] Against such charges versatile Louis Houck, former editor and state historian, managed to portray himself as a rugged individualist fighting mighty forces—corporations and unconstitutional legislation and judicial interpretation.[4] Then, too, his other avocations such as stimulation of community education and devotion to literary pursuits, in that they were generally conducted with philanthropic showmanship, had the effect of minimizing Houck's financial interests.[5]

Seven years before Houck became a railroad director, he demonstrated his enthusiasm for transportation by acquiring in 1872 a majority of stock in the Cape Girardeau and Scott County McAdamized Road.[6] This company had been chartered in 1853 with the exclusive privilege of constructing a macadamized road across the "Big Swamp" in the counties of Cape Girardeau and Scott.[7] It was but one of approximately sixty road companies granted charters by the Missouri legislature between the years 1835 and 1865, when "private capital toyed with developing roads in a fashion akin to later railway development."[8]

In order to attract necessary money, certain liberal provisions were incorporated in the company's charter. County courts of Cape Girardeau and Scott were authorized to invest county funds in the stock of the company if desired; such stock was deemed and held as personal property, exempt from all taxes for state or county purposes; and specified rates were enumerated. For example, the charge allowed for a wagon or vehicle drawn by six animals was sixty-five cents; for a man and a horse, ten cents.[9] Most important in later controversies was section 8, which stated that privileges granted in original charters continued for fifty years, provided that county courts at the expiration of twenty years, or any time thereafter, purchased said roads at actual cost of construction and eliminated the tolls.

"Big Swamp" had its origin in Scott County below Cape Girardeau, and the company acquired the right to build a road across it for a distance of three or four miles, with an additional privilege of extending the crossing to the city.[10] As the road eventually was located on a levee, it became known as the Rock Levee Road. However, completion of the toll road to Cape Girardeau was not accomplished until 1873, when Louis Houck became the company's new president. According to Houck, an extension had suddenly become vital. Since Cape Girardeau was excluded from the Iron Mountain Railway, securing Scott County business was essential to the city's prosperity.[11] Such reasoning was remarkably similar to Houck's explanations for railroad building a decade later. Before extension of the toll road, the only approach for travelers to the city from Scott and New Madrid counties had been over an almost impassable mud road.

In an address before an immigration convention at Cape Girardeau in July, 1889, Houck cited his faith in cheap transportation as an indication of material and intellectual growth of a country. He declared,

> Our road laws are framed to encourage the construction of good and substantial roads, but farmers and business men do not give the subject the attention and thought it deserves. Somebody must see to it that the taxes and labor are intellectually expended.[12]

This benevolent opinion expressed by the toll road director was delivered prior to passage of a law April 3, 1901, which stated that control and management of all graveled or macadamized roads of the state whose charter life had expired, or was to expire, passed to and was vested in the county court of the county in which the road was situated.[13] Accordingly, it was the duty of the prosecuting and circuit attorneys of respective counties or circuits through which such roads ran to enjoin, restrain, and prohibit any corporation which kept possession and control of the roads by the collection of tolls.

In an effort to circumvent this ruling, Houck attempted to gain permanent possession of the toll road property by organizing a new company to take over the old company's property. On May 26, 1903, the Scott County Macadamized Road Company filed articles of incorporation; on May 27, 1903, Louis Houck, president of the old Cape Girardeau and Scott County Macadamized Road Company, conveyed to the new Scott County Macadamized Road Company all real estate, property assets, rights, franchises, including roadbed, right-of-way and toll gates.

Litigation, a persistent feature in Houck's career, resulted. The case against the toll road was evidently underwritten by the Commercial Club of Cape Girardeau, an organization which played a Chamber of Commerce role in the city's development and prosperity.[15] As one local newspaper later phrased the struggle, "No sooner did the opportunity come than the Commercial Club of Cape Girardeau got busy and through long litigation took Mr. Houck's road away from him without paying him a cent for it."[16]

When the toll road case reached Missouri's Supreme Court, Houck lawyers based most of their fight on the interpretation of the original charter's wording.[17] Houck's legal battery emphasized that in the original act of incorporation the macadamized road company "may and shall have perpetual succession as such, and may make and use a common seal, and the same to alter at pleasure." In addition to the argument based on "perpetual succession" phraseology, Houck claimed that the company was being deprived of property without due process of law; before their property could be taken from them, the owners would have to be compensated for construction expense.

The Missouri Supreme Court made short shrift of these contentions. If legal existence of a corporation whose charter granted it "perpetual succession" was by another section limited to fifty years, "perpetual succession" meant limited but not eternal existence. The court flatly denied that the company was being deprived of property rights. "The grant of the privilege to collect tolls from travelers upon the public highway limited its compensation to its right to collect tolls, and that right having expired the road became a free public highway," stated the justices. "Thereafter, the public has a right to use the road without paying tolls or compensating the corporation or its stockholders for the expense it incurred in macadamizing or otherwise constructing the turnpike." However, the court ruled that the state could not appropriate toll gates, toll houses, and other property used by the company in collecting tolls. Just what use Houck could make of these, without the accompanying road, the court declined to state.

By this time, local papers had begun their editorial remarks on the subject of toll roads. On June 15, 1907, the *Cape Girardeau Democrat* predicted, "Toll gates have long since been knocked out in all counties in Missouri except Cape Girardeau and now we are to get in line with civilization." On June 22, 1907, the paper impatiently queried, "The toll roads are still collecting toll. What's the matter with the Supreme Court?" On July 13, 1907, there was reported the case of an impatient farmer who chopped down the toll gate of the Jackson Gravel Road, another toll road which existed in the county and was undergoing legal controversies similar to Houck's road.[18] According to the paper, this road company "will now use iron bars instead of wooden poles" in withstanding the nonpaying users of the road.

The Supreme Court of Missouri had rendered its decision November 6, 1907. Two years later the Supreme Court of the United States reaffirmed the state court's decision.[19] In the nation's highest tribunal, Houck forces refined their argument that the company could not be deprived of its right to take tolls except by a purchase of the road at the actual cost of construction. They stressed that provision for right to purchase at the expiration of twenty years or any time thereafter meant the right to make the road free. Even after fifty years, toll exemption could be gained only by purchase. Such provision, it was declared, constituted contract and created property rights beyond the power of a state to impair or to take away. In a decision written by Associate Justice Oliver Wendell Holmes, the court decided that all privileges of the road corporation ceased at the end of fifty years, that the owner of the franchise was not deprived of his property without due process of law, and that no obligation of contract was impaired by an injunction against the company brought by the local prosecuting attorney.

In his memoirs, Houck brushed off defeat by stating that courts misconstrued the word "perpetual." Declaring that the property had cost him in excess of $30,000 "on which not a dollar has been repaid in the way of dividends or otherwise," he fittingly concluded: "But the courts finally adjudicate the rights of parties and in the opinion of most people the courts are infallible. There is no such thing as judicial larceny."[20]

A decade after the litigation had ended, the fate of Louis Houck's toll road reappeared for consideration in connection with Houck's opposition to Cape Girardeau's approval of a million dollar five per cent bond issue for "good roads." According to the Cape Girardeau Southeast Missourian,

Houck could be excused for opposing the bond issue because he had built a fine pike, had made no profits because small tolls were charged, and had kept the road in perfect condition all the time.[21] Since the gates had been torn down, the road had been in deplorable condition. Some toll roads were in reality public property because public highways had been turned over to private corporations to be operated as toll roads. But, asserted the paper, the road built by Houck was not a public highway when he created it, and it was constructed on private property. Actually the Missouri Supreme Court had offered much documentary evidence and testimony of witnesses on the question of whether a public highway had existed along the route of the road prior to 1851. Although no records were available showing establishment of a county road by order of the county court, the Supreme Court interpreted the evidence presented as showing that the portion of the road crossing the "Big Swamp," or what was known as the rock levee, was utilized by the public prior to the construction of this toll road. The Supreme Court also noted that right-of-way for a part of the last constructed road was obtained by condemnation proceedings. It did not appear, stated the court, that the Cape Girardeau and Scott County McAdamized Road Company had ever obtained any portion of the right-of-way by any kind of deed of conveyance, except in one instance.

A decade after the case against Louis Houck's toll road had been determined, Louis Houck offered, in paid advertisements, arguments against Cape Girardeau's voting bond issues for "good roads."[22] He recalled the debt Girardeans contracted on their original railroad indebtedness; he was cognizant of the fact that roads did not pay taxes as railroads did; and he warned that when roads needed improvement, taxpayers would be charged for necessary maintenance. To Houck, agents of bond houses of big cities were the instigators of such schemes, and their bonds, he warned, would not sell at par. That an ex-toll road director would voice such sentiments was not surprising. According to the Missouri Planning Board, toll road executives "were responsible to some extent for the notion that, if good roads were to be built and maintained, the undertaking had to be sponsored by the particular local area affected rather than by the country at large."

In an evaluation of the toll road company's role, the board stated:

> These private corporations definitely diluted the responsibility of the county courts in road matters just as the organized township and special road districts do today. Thus, they germinated the idea of a completely decentralized road administration and authority which became the trend after 1870.[23]

The Cape Girardeau paper, disposing of the controversy over toll roads, and accepting the burning issue of "good roads," likened Houck's predicament to that of another lost cause in the first quarter of the twentieth century:

> Every reform and every great movement for good works a hardship upon certain people. Take for instance the whiskey makers. The law permitted them to make whiskey and then all of a sudden the law said they could not sell it. Men were left with their every dollar invested in whiskey. Those who were responsible for the changed law contended that while a few would suffer the very great majority would profit by it.
>
> While Mr. Houck was probably mistreated in the road matter, it won't do to stop the progress of the entire country.[24]

In the last quarter of his life, Louis Houck had occasion to warn citizens of his community against voting bond issues for good roads, for municipal water and electric light plants,[25] and for the Little River Drainage organization, which had been formed for the purpose of draining swamp lands of southeast Missouri. In 1909 Houck first publicly took issue with the formation of the Little River Drainage District, because he felt that the proposition to build a diversion channel to carry off creek water into the Mississippi River about two miles south of Cape Girardeau would create more swamps in the county.[26] Houck often called attention to the fact that promoters of the scheme, particularly the International

Harvester and Himmelberger-Harrison lumber interests, had not included their land within the drainage district. He charged that the best farm lands of Cape Girardeau and Bollinger counties had been incorporated for purposes of creating an attractive market for the issue and sale of bonds to investors. The next year Houck canvassed southeast Missouri with speeches against Little River drainage districting.

On July 12, 1911, Houck wrote the *St. Louis Republic* on the "drainage craze" that had hit Missouri.[27] In a lengthy letter he characterized the drainage movement as one of several "periodic abberations" afflicting Missourians, comparable to the township railroad subscription craze in 1868. Houck identified promoters of the drainage craze generally as real estate speculators, contractors, bond houses, and bond lawyers. Recent general assemblies of Missouri, Houck maintained, "induced by the specious plea that the state must be fully improved quickly, the land drained quickly, the empty places filled up quickly, the last tree cut down quickly . . ." had swept away constitutional guarantees by their drainage laws.

Houck went on record as opposed to laws which provided that in certain drainage districts organized by circuit courts, owners of a majority of acres would have control of the district and elect the supervisors. As these supervisors were not necessarily residents of the district on which bonds were issued, they represented principles which were "undemocratic and monarchical, and contrary to every principle of free government." That property of small owners would be confiscated under this law was demonstrated, Houck contended, by a report of commissioners of the Little River Drainage District: "where land that had been in cultivation for one hundred years and producing good crops is assessed as being benefited as much by the contemplated drainage work as land that has been a swamp and under water since the world began."

Rather dismally Houck concluded:

> I realize that it is useless to protest. It is useless
> to designate the individuals promoting these flag-

rant and confiscatory schemes. The sinister purpose is understood, at least in this section, by all thinking men. But when a craze takes possession of the public mind all office seekers and officeholders get in the band wagon. When the catastrophe comes, as it is sure to come in this "drainage craze" no one will remember that he rode in the wagon; everybody will be innocent, and the swindled people only will be the sufferers.

In turn, the *St. Louis Republic* recalled that the federal government had expended tens of millions in reclamation of arid lands. When these had been reduced to cultivation, they did not approach in productive value the reclaimed swamp and submerged lands of Missouri.[28] The paper believed that Houck's fears would be allayed when reclamation proceeded with due regard to conservative business methods, and that large development projects afforded no opportunity for "financial buccaneering," as in an earlier era.

Another metropolitan paper, perceiving that people living in a vast area from Missouri to the Gulf were below the standard in physical condition, commented that "it would not seem possible to pay too high a price for the remedying of such a condition—though, of course, the price should be equitably assessed as possible."[29] It was conceded that reclamation should possibly be handled nationally, rather than locally. But either way, the paper believed that the drainage craze was the most advantageous craze the country had experienced in a century.

The *St. Louis Republic*, July 29, 1911, opened its columns to Otto Kochtitzky, engineer of the Little River Drainage District, for rebuttal purposes. "Local sentiment demands drainage," charged the engineer, "and it is useless for mossbacks to resist or for drones to hope to ride without paying." According to Kochtitzky,

> the drainage cost is not looked upon by the land owners as a tax, but as an investment, and is considered as part of the price of the land. Thus on lands worth $1 per acre to $4 per acre, by fastening a lien of $8 or $10 in ditch assessments per acre, we

have been able to create a value of $30 to $50 per acre.

Ownership of land had remained largely in possession of the original promoters of reclamation, stated Kochtitzky, "because the property is worth the price and we do not know where to reinvest the money to better advantage."

Houck managed to have the last printed word before the Little River Drainage District was an accomplished fact.[30] Houck contended that Kochtitzky was laboring under the impression that because particular schemes of drainage were objectionable, opposition had been made to reasonable and sane methods of drainage promoting the section's prosperity. Six specific charges were made by Houck against this particular scheme. First, the "drainage craze" was being "pulled off" in Missouri by people who owned no land in the drainage district. Second, the "craze" was tearing down constitutional bulwarks. Third, Kochtitzky had failed to recall earlier and unsuccessful reclamation projects. Houck remembered that as payment for reclamation work, New Madrid County once issued patents for approximately 165,000 acres of land worth millions for the timber alone, though he stated that the land was substantially as wet as ever when the project was finished. The total consequences, maintained Houck, was that contractors set up one of the largest sawmill plants of the country, made millions out of timber, and sold whatever land they could. The timber was now gone and the sawmill about to be dismantled. Houck contended that such factors explained the new Little River Drainage plan, as these original contractors, Deering of the International Harvester Company, and other allied interests, made up the majority of the owners of acreage. Fourth, Houck argued against the district's geographical formation, charging, in effect, gerrymandering on the part of the Deering crowd. Fifth, Houck believed that the "beauty of the plan" of cutting a ditch below Cape Girardeau which was expected to discharge the waters of about 1,200 to 1,500 square miles of the Ozark hills would be "appreciated" when it was remembered that the Mississippi River got bank full, and more, every year. Sixth, Houck doubted that the assessment of benefits would equal the selling price of reclaimed land within a generation.

Such newspaper arguments represented only the beginning of Houck's fight against the Little River Drainage District. Having expressed himself in Missouri papers, Houck's disgruntlement found further outlet via the courts, opening the second phase of the battle.[31] One of Missouri's drainage laws, authorizing a drainage district to collect a tax of twenty-five cents per acre for costs of preliminary organizational expenses, was the impetus for a series of court decisions involving Houck and the drainage district.[32] Seeking to prevent collection of such tax, and asking that an injunction be granted to prevent the collector from selling their property because of their failure and refusal to pay such tax, Houck and others brought suit in the Common Pleas Court of Cape Girardeau in 1910. The case was not tried in the local court because the drainage district, on a change of venue, carried it to the Cape Girardeau Circuit Court. The Little River Drainage District filed a demurrer on grounds that facts sufficient for a cause of action had not been stated in the taxpayers' petition. When the circuit court decided the demurrer in favor of the district, the Houcks appealed to the State Supreme Court. Both sides agreed that the one question to be settled was the constitutionality of the section which provided for collection of such tax.[33]

In brief, the court upheld the constitutionality of drainage laws applicable to the Little River Drainage District. It acknowledged the right of the state to create corporations in prescribed districts for purposes of reclaiming or improving swamp and submerged lands by ditches, drains, and levees. The Supreme Court held that right to tax in such cases was a matter of government concern because lands of the state were increased in productiveness and value and the wealth and comfort of the people were promoted. Houck had attacked the tax for preliminary organization work on grounds that no judicial finding of benefits was required by law as a foundation for levying such assessments. The court decided that preliminary work was for purposes of relieving those found to receive the least benefit from the execution of the contemplated plan. In addition, preliminary organization afforded necessary data whereby costs were imposed upon those who ought in equity to bear it. In answer to Houck's charge that there might be no resulting increment which under the name of "benefits" constituted the only constitutional approach for this class of taxation, the court replied that it was not within its province to find fault with legislative reasoning, "and if it were, we doubt whether we could substitute a more equitable plan."

Holding that all work, whether purely preliminary or purely constructive, was necessary for fulfillment of the purposes of the drainage district, the Supreme Court of Missouri considered the prosperity and growth of productive communities represented by farms as matters of general public concern. "That concern," stated the court, "is represented by the difference between a State composed of bogs and marshes not only unproductive but unhealthy, and a State in which the lands yield bountifully to the call of the husbandman, and breathe health instead of miasma."[34]

The case of Houck versus the Little River Drainage District extended from one court to another with the inevitable prediction that Louis Houck might petition the Hague tribunal.[35] However, the decision of the Supreme Court of the United States written by Associate Justice Charles Evans Hughes was in effect the final affirmation of the state supreme court's decision.[36]

Having lost the battle with newspapers and courts, Houck's next method of attack was to sponsor laws unfavorable to the drainage district. The impetus for Cape Girardeau County's election of Major Giboney Houck to the Missouri House of Representatives in 1918 was a series of Missouri Supreme Court decisions maintaining that the burden of building bridges over canals cut through a county's road system was on the county and not on the drainage district which did the cutting.[37] Giboney Houck was elected by voters on his pledge to have the drainage laws amended so as to relieve the people of Cape Girardeau County from the cost of building bridges across the Little River diversion channel.[38] Giboney Houck, only elected Democrat from the county in that year, had heavily advertised his candidacy in the Cape Girardeau paper. In paid advertisements containing Supreme Court extracts, Louis Houck had explained to taxpayers that the only relief from bridge expenses was not from the courts, but from legislative action.[39] However, the "Houck-Speer" bill, devoted to the above purpose, failed of passage. Expensive lobbying, plus loss of previously pledged votes from city representatives, became the explanation in rural Missouri.[40] As in his earlier railroad litigation, Houck spent the last fifteen years of his life in futile battle with the Little River Drainage District.[41] The Little River Drainage District in turn offered its most convincing rebuttal by its report of increase in the valuation of southeast Missouri lands.[42]

Louis Houck had lived a long time. In the earlier period of his life it was he who was hailed as the promoter of his section's prosperity for having built the necessary short-line railroads to serve as outlets for the timber products of his region. And it was he who had attempted to obtain the rewards of reclamation by constructing the levees for his roads, only to meet the disapproval of the courts. When it came to the surrender of his pike, and the assessment of his lands for cost of drainage by an "outside" organization, Louis Houck's experiences in the latter part of the nineteenth century had left him unprepared for the "progressive" sentiments underscored by press and bar in the first quarter of the twentieth century. Doggedly he continued to fight in the legendary Houck manner: endless litigation, preachments to the press, and political action.

NOTES TO CHAPTER IV

[1] *St. Louis Post-Dispatch,* February 21, 1925, and June 1, 1929; *St. Louis Star,* February 21, 1925.

[2] See Frederick H. Brennan's feature story, "By Louis Houck—a School, Six Books, 500 Miles of Railroad, Only Man Who Ever Beat Jay Gould in a Deal," *St. Louis Post-Dispatch,* March 1, 1925.

[3] *St. Louis Republic,* July 29, 1911.

[4] *St. Louis Republic,* July 12, 21, 29, and August 1, 1911.

[5] *Southeast Missourian* (Cape Girardeau, Missouri), February 18, 1925.

[6] Louis Houck, "Reminiscences" [Cape Girardeau, Missouri, n.d.], p. 229.

[7] *Laws of Missouri* (1852-1853), pp. 337-8.

[8] *Local Road Administration in Missouri, an Interpretation in terms of its historical development* (Jefferson City, Missouri, July, 1936), pp. 30-5.

[9] *Cape Girardeau Democrat,* May 27, 1893.

[10] *Southeast Missouri State College Alumni Bulletin* (Cape Girardeau, Missouri, October 14-15, 1949).

[11] Houck, "Reminiscences," p. 231.

[12] Louis Houck scrapbook [Cape Girardeau, Missouri, n.d., n.p].

[13] *Laws of Missouri* (1901), pp. 235-6.

[14] *Missouri Reports,* CCVII (1907), 54-85.

[15] Allan H. Hinchey, "The Commercial Club," *Educational Outlook,* I, No. 1 (Cape Girardeau, Missouri, April, 1913), 25-27.

[16] *Cape Girardeau Southeast Missourian,* December 12, 1919.

[17] "The State *ex rel.* Hines, Prosecuting Attorney, vs. Scott County Macadamized Road Company, Appellant," *Missouri Reports,* CCVII, 54-85.

[18] "The State *ex rel.* Hines, Prosecuting Attorney, vs. the Cape Girardeau and Jackson Gravel Road Company," *Missouri Reports,* CCVII, 85-107.

[19] "Scott County Macadamized Road Company vs. State of Missouri *ex rel.* Hines, Prosecuting Attorney of Cape Girardeau County," *United States Reports,* CCXV, 336-41.

[20] Houck, "Reminiscences," p. 234.

[21] *Cape Girardeau Southeast Missourian,* December 12, 1919.

[22] *Ibid.*

[23] *Local Road Administration in Missouri,* p. 35.

[24] *Cape Girardeau Southeast Missourian,* December 12, 1919.

[25] *Weekly Republican* (Cape Girardeau, Missouri), September 27, 1912.

[26] *Daily Republican* (Cape Girardeau, Missouri), December 9, 1909.

[27] Also see *Daily Republican,* December 9, 1909.

[28] *St. Louis Republic,* July 13, 1911.

[29] *St. Louis Times,* reprinted in *Weekly Republican* (Cape Girardeau, Missouri), July 14, 1911.

[30] *St. Louis Republic,* August 1, 1911.

[31] *Weekly Republican,* October 29, 1915, carried a review of litigation.

[32] *Laws of Missouri* (1909), p. 629; *Revised Statutes of Missouri* (1909), section 5538.

[33] "Louis Houck, *et al.,* Appellants vs. Little River Drainage District *et al.,*" *Missouri Reports,* CCXLVIII, 373-94.

[34] *Ibid.*

[35] *Weekly Republican,* October 29, 1915. Also see addenda to *Bulletin of the Little River Drainage District,* No. 5, November, 1915.

[36] "Houck vs. Little River Drainage District," *United States Reports,* CCXXXIX, 254-67.

[37] See particularly, "The State *ex rel.* John McWilliams, Prosecuting Attorney of Scott County, Appellant, vs. Little River Drainage District, *et al., Missouri Reports,* CCLXIX, 444-63, and "The State *ex rel.* J. Henry Caruthers, Prosecuting Attorney of Cape Girardeau County, Appellant, vs. Little River Drainage District," *Missouri Reports,* CCLXXI, 429-37. These cases substantiated the idea that drainage districts were public corporations devoted to public purposes; that as custodians of the highways within its district, county courts were but agents of the state; and that the burden of bridge expenses fell on the county, but not on the drainage district. While the cost of building a bridge seemed a hard injustice upon the county, the court said the remedy lay only within the control of the legislative branch of the state government.

[38] *Cape Girardeau Southeast Missourian,* November 1, 1918.

[39] *Ibid.,* November 1, December 20, 1918; January 3, February 7, February 14, February 21, March 21, and April 11, 1919.

[40] *Ibid.,* April 25, 1919.

[41] See case entitled "Little River Drainage District, Respondent, vs. Louis Houck and Mary G. Houck, Appellants," *Missouri Appeal Reports,* CCXXCII, 283-7, for evidences of continual friction between the two sides.

[42] According to *Bulletin of Little River Drainage District,* No. 18, February, 1919, the assessed valuation of all lands in the district in Cape Girardeau County in 1910 was $262,845. In 1918, it was $1,188,-085, constituting an increase in valuation of 354 per cent.

In 1910 the assessed valuation for state and county purposes on lands in Cape Girardeau County in the drainage district north of the Headwater Diversion Channel was $90,549. In 1918 the valuation on the same lands was $197,416, or an increase in valuation of 118 per cent.

Lands south of the Diversion Channel in Cape Girardeau County which were assessed a benefit increased 660 per cent, and all lands south of the channel increased 475 per cent.

CHAPTER V

INSTITUTIONAL PROMOTIONS IN THE MISSOURI BOOTHEEL: PRISON, LIBRARY AND COLLEGE

"I don't say anything about the injustice done to Southeast Missouri. Our part of the State has sucked the hind teat so long that we are accustomed to scant rations."—Cape Girardean writing in the *St. Louis Post-Dispatch*, July 8, 1885.

IN A MESSAGE of January 7, 1885, to the Missouri legislature, Governor Thomas J. Crittenden suggested building an additional state penitentiary.[1] The chief executive stressed the need for "mature" consideration because Missouri's single state prison, located at Jefferson City, the capital, boasted an unenviable record of housing the largest number of prisoners in the nation, with the exception of Sing Sing, New York. Missouri newspapers quickly acquiesced to the Governor's recommendation by stressing the crowding of fifteen hundred convicts within the walls of the state prison.[2] Moreover, editors warned their readers to expect an increase to two thousand prisoners in the near future. Those acquainted with penal reform elsewhere viewed the existing situation as intolerable. One hundred cells contained five men each, and others contained as many as four. As a means of relieving congestion and instituting reform programs for prisoners, many reformers favored construction of a branch prison to house convicts of "the better class, or old ones whose time is nearly out."

The governor's recommendation that the branch penitentiary be built adjacent to a railroad and near some prosperous business city naturally aroused the competitive instincts of Missouri towns. In turn, the legislature responded favorably to the will of citizens vitally concerned with reform and also with enhancement of local real estate values. On March 30, 1885, the chief executive had the pleasure of signing an act providing for Missouri Penitentiary No. 2, which realized his original ideas on the subject.[3] The search now began for a site "with a view to the health of the prisoners, and so located as to afford the best facilities for obtaining material for the employment of the labor of the convicts and contiguous to a good market for the products of such labor. . . ."[4] Price for such location was not to exceed $20,000, and final payment necessitated approval of three inspectors: John Walker, state auditor (Howard County); James Seibert, state treasurer (Cape Girardeau County); and Banton G. Boone, attorney general (Henry County).[5]

Louis Houck, by virtue of his legal and railroading activities, quickly sensed opportunities for himself and his city. As he later expressed his motivation, "My interest then in the railroad operated from Wayne County to Cape Girardeau was such that anything that promised an increase of business was of great interest to me."[6] Under testimony he expanded his interest to include not only an increase in his railroad's business, but also a rise in the value of his and Mrs. Houck's ownership of some twelve thousand acres of land within a radius of nine miles of Cape Girardeau; of this land, six to seven thousand acres were within a radius of three to four miles of the city, and four hundred acres and additional lots were within the city. The Houcks also owned some eight to ten thousand acres in the adjoining county of Scott.[7]

Prodded by the railroad king of southeast Missouri, citizens of Cape Girardeau made commendable efforts to obtain the institution. A display in the Missouri Senate chamber revealed a large and varied assortment of Cape Girardeau County products: granite, potter's clay, fire clay, ochre, and silica. So impressed was a Jefferson City newspaperman that he reported:

> The county in the neighborhood of Cape Girardeau is well provided with granite quarries, and in fact everything necessary for utilized [sic] either rough or skilled labor. The Board of prison inspectors have

taken a great deal of pains to carefully examined
[sic] all the competing localities and it does not
appear that any place has presented more favorable
inducements then [sic] Cape Girardeau.[8]

The news account seemed neither ill-timed nor over-stated.
The board agreed to an option on Houck property fronting
the river. That versatile propagandist, who had spent several
weeks lobbying in Jefferson City for the site, "celebrated the
victory by, as was customary then, setting up drinks and
champagne in the Madison Hotel."[9]

Festivities were premature. Criticism immediately manifested itself in the Missouri press when Cape Girardeau was
adjudged the winner. Only the La Grange Democrat seemed
disinterested in its comment:

Cape Girardeau captured the branch penitentiary.
What it is going to do with it now that it has it is
the current conundrum. At the risk of going to the
penitentiary we are constrained to say that if it
keeps on catching institutions it will in due time
be as "ornery" a town as some other boroughs now
similarly blessed. Thank goodness LaGrange didn't
get it! It got the measles, mumps, and Missouri
mange this spring, and that was as much as our
Calamity Jane could care for one season.[10]

The St. Louis Post-Dispatch pondered the selection because
there had been general understanding that the penitentiary
would be located at Kansas City.[11] The Moberly Headlight
flatly stated that the committee had offered $20,000 for one
hundred acres of land not worth over $3 per acre, and de-
clared that Moberly would gladly have furnished sufficient
land for $5,000.[12] The State Journal attempted arbitration
between Moberly and Cape Girardeau:

So far as the city of Moberly and Randolph County
are concerned, it must be admitted they are vastly
superior to Cape Girardeau in point of enterprise,
value, and accessibility. As we understand the matter, the prison was located at Cape Girardeau on
account of the vast amount of raw material which
could easily be obtained and always afford employment for the convicts. The tract of land is inside the

corporate limits of the city and we are given to understand that it is worth the price paid.[13]

However, the *St. Louis Post-Dispatch* kept alive the doubts concerning the selection of Houck property by rounding up all adverse opinions from the state press:

> It is conceded on all hands that Treasurer Seibert stood up for his own corner of the State like a man, but he is told that he should have declined to pass as a judge upon a matter in which he and his whole town were so deeply interested. For voting with Seibert, Auditor Walker is prodded with divers and sundry and cruel imputations. The *Moberly Headlight* says he worked hard for Kansas City and would have given the prize to her "but the owners of the site could not agree on a division of the $20,-000 to be paid for the land." The *Richmond Democrat* also intimates that Cape Girardeau got it because Kansas City folks "refused to make a special effort"—whatever that may be. The *Louisiana Press* suspects something bigger than a mere "divvy" in the land sale, and talks about an Anchor Line and railroad ring arrangement in the interest of Colonel Griff Prather and Mr. Houck, and also in the interest of Auditor Walker's race for the Gubernatorial nomination in 1888.[14]

The *Post-Dispatch* reminded its readers that Auditor Walker, a member of the State Board of Equalization, had assessed Cape Girardeau land at five dollars an acre. Now he valued the same property at $200 an acre when commissioned to buy it for the state.

L. J. Albert, president of the Cape Girardeau Board of Trade and executive of one of the Houck railroad companies, quickly defended the choice of the inspectors:

> The proposed site for the branch Penitentiary in our city is situated within three quarters mile of our Court House, fronts on the Mississippi River and affords a fine landing for steamboats; the railroad connecting with the entire Southwestern system runs through the tract at the foot of the hill; the site is underlaid with fine quarries of blue limestone and the celebrated Cape Girardeau marble, out of which

the Louisiana State House was erected, and in short, is one of the noblest building sites on the river between St. Louis and New Orleans.[15]

Newspaper readers of the state were treated to an eloquent retort by the *Moberly Headlight*:

> Of course, the State should not overlook or underestimate the importance of having a "noble building site" for the delectation of its convicts. It will be so grateful to their senses to gaze out on the tranquil bosom of the Father of Waters as he rolls on majestically toward the sea. It is also well to have the site underlaid with a solid strata of limestone, as otherwise the muskrats from the river might burrow up inside the walls, and thus open an avenue of escape for the prisoners.[16]

The *Fredericktown Standard* intimated that with the $20,000 paid for the hundred-acre farm, Houck could now extend his railroad operations ten miles further into the unknown of southeast Missouri, and rout the alligators and mosquitoes in that swampy section of the state.[17] The *St. Louis Post-Dispatch* castigated Auditor Walker for a speech made at Fredericktown, in which he suggested that to obtain a branch penitentiary a town must find responsible parties who would undertake to work three hundred convicts for a term of years at sixty cents per day. "The inspectors," said the paper, with obvious reference to Houck interests, "without intending it perhaps, have somehow sent abroad an impression that the convicts were to be hired out to work in mines and quarries, to work on railroads, get out cross-ties, clear forest, and drain them."[18]

In the midst of newspaper accusations in the summer of 1885,[19] the commissioners reversed their unanimous decision for Cape Girardeau as the penitentiary site. Various explanations for their decision were forthcoming. According to the *St. Louis Post-Dispatch*, the commissioners declared they could make no purchase at the Cape until land owners proved by more reliable and numerous affidavits that the selling price of the land was not exorbitant.[20] Later testimony revealed that upon a return inspection trip to the Houck property, the commissioners had found a large portion of the land flooded from recent rain.[21] In his memoirs, Houck suggested that failure to pay $5,000 to unidentified parties accounted for the cancellation.[22] According to Houck, William Brown, a business associate, was informed by a professor of Washington University, St. Louis, that unless such sum was paid, location would be cancelled and the institution located elsewhere. Still another explanation for Cape Girardeau's failure was "its geographic situation to the state and its distance from a good market."[23]

So embittered was an anonymous Girardean by the cancellation of his town as the site for the new prison, that he wrote the *St. Louis Post-Dispatch* of the harm it had caused both cities—Cape Girardeau and St. Louis.[24] Intimating to the newspaper that Kansas City might now be selected, the reader suggested that St. Louisans would not be allowed to supply as much as a toothpick for the warden's teeth. Charging an ignorant lack of sectional self-interest by the paper, the Girardean suggested that the Houck site would have meant that St. Louis would have realized profit from every dollar's worth of supplies and every pound of iron furnished the institution.[25]

During the year of 1885 several Missouri towns suffered Cape Girardeau's fate.[26] It seemed as if many were called, but none was chosen by the inspectors. Branch Penitentiary No. 2 was said to have acquired a history similar to that of "the fabled Wandering Jew, it keeps traveling."[27] Cape Girardeau, Kansas City, Louisiana, Hannibal, St. Joseph, and Moberly all figured prominently in the contest. Finally one newspaper asserted that the penitentiary commissioners

> do not claim to be unable to decide which is the best site, but the question dearer by far to them is "Will the people elect us again if we decide?" We think, gentlemen, you are gone anyway. An honest decision would not have prejudiced the people, but your vacillating has.[28]

In a statesman-like manner, the *State Journal* finally pointed the way out of difficulty. Its platform became: one prison and one management under daily supervision and direction of the inspectors.[29] On August 21, 1885, the capital city's newspaper happily reported that necessary moves had been made to enlarge the penitentiary at Jefferson City.

The governor and his commissioners undoubtedly were politically embarrassed by the situation. The affront to civic pride, as well as the name calling of one Missouri town by another, boded ill for any administration. A larger problem, however, overshadowed the prison controversy: that of railroad control. Newspapers began to utilize the penitentiary fiasco primarily as a weapon against Walker, who was under severe criticism as a railroad assessor, and against Houck, a small railroad director who was opposed to stricter governmental regulation of transportation.[30] Inevitably, Houck's techniques for securing an institution for his city were compared with his business methods in short-line railway construction.[31]

The next session of the Missouri legislature authorized an investigation of the state auditor, John Walker, on various counts.[32] One count charged that in consideration of money offered him by Louis Houck and others, Walker had voted to locate the branch penitentiary at Cape Girardeau. It was disclosed by Houck's testimony that he had agreed to pay Colonel J. R. Willis (ex-warden who was appointed head of the branch penitentiary) a commission equivalent to 15 or 17 per cent of the $20,000 for whatever help Willis rendered in the procurement of the prison at Cape Girardeau.[33] Although Houck stated that he did not know whether Willis was actually responsible for Walker's vote for Cape Girardeau, he testified that he was "suspicious" of Walker. Houck's arrangements with Willis had been made on a Saturday, and the following Monday Walker first voted for Cape Girardeau. However, it was the opinion of the investigating committee that Walker acted without knowledge or notice of a money consideration.[34]

Upon these disclosures, the *St. Louis Post-Dispatch* felt compelled to harken back to its fight with Houck by suggesting that the Missouri governor had it in his power to strike a telling blow in the interests of honesty, decency, reform, and political purity by punishing rascals who had raised such a fund.[35] Even a newspaper friendly to Houck, the *Republican*, embarking upon a crusade for railroad regulation, stated that "the Mr. Louis Houck mentioned as a party to the above bargain was the same Mr. Louis Houck who had been actively interested against railroad regulation." The findings of the investigating committee, stated the paper, "gives a very fair idea of his methods."[36]

Undoubtedly as a consequence of the Walker investigations, the act creating Penitentiary No. 2 was repealed on March 22, 1887.[37] Yet there remained evidence that Louis Houck, in the midst of accusations, still entertained ideas of locating the prison at Cape Girardeau. In that same session of the legislature, Senator Madison R. Smith and Representative R. H. Whitelaw, southeast Missourians friendly to Houck, introduced bills in their respective chambers for the establishment of a branch prison.[38] But Missouri preferred to remain a "one penitentiary" state. Houck's insistence on keeping up the struggle, against impossible odds, only underscored the famous trait of persistency he was then displaying in his fight against governmental transportation regulation and in his tortuous railroad controversies with the Goulds.

Perhaps the real value of the lost struggle to Houck was that it made him aware of the need for more favorable portrayal by newspapers in the state. In the future, better press relations were achieved two ways. Houck accentuated his role as a rugged individualist fighting the larger corporate railroad forces in Missouri. He became a patron of the "self-help" institutions of his city.

As chief executive, Governor Marmaduke had the power to appease zealous Girardeans involved in promoting institutions. He nominated Houck member of the Board of Regents of the Southeast Missouri Normal School in 1886.[39] The appointee continued as an official of the board until his death, serving as its president from 1889 to 1925.[40] Actually, Houck's interest in the institution dated from 1873, when the Missouri legislature passed an act for the establishment of a normal school in an undetermined place in the southeastern section of the state;[41] he became an original promoter of the city's subscription bond to capture the institution.[42] In addition he offered ten acres of land, free of cost, in an historical setting near Fort "D," a Civil War fortification. The regents favored Fort "B," however, not only because at the highest elevation in the city, college buildings would be visible from afar, but also because students would be protected from malaria emanating from the lowlands of southeast Missouri.

At the time of Houck's appointment, the main accomplishment of the board was the erection of one building characterized as "a perfect beauty in architectural design."[43] But to Houck it was "an architectural excrescence, which had fortunately been destroyed by fire in 1902."[44] In descriptive agreement was another Missourian, Mark Twain, who had written in 1883:

> Cape Girardeau is situated on a hillside and makes for a handsome appearance. There is a great Jesuit school for boys at the foot of the town by the river. Uncle Mumford said it has as high a reputation for thoroughness as any similar institution in Missouri. There was another college high up on an airy summit —a bright new edifice, picturesquely and peculiarly towered and pinnacled—a sort of gigantic casters, with the cruets all complete.[45]

Mark Twain felt constrained to add that partialities often made people see more than really existed. There can be little argument that Houck was partial to this institution, and that he saw potentialities for growth beyond its one building. When Houck first entered upon his duties as a board member there were nine teachers, 278 students, one building, and nine acres of campus. At Houck's death, faculty and staff consisted of sixty persons, there were 1,000 students, and the campus and grounds had been enlarged to 190 acres, on which sat seven monumental stone buildings.[46]

That a heavily propertied constructor of railroads would be interested in an improvement of the physical assets of

the state college was not surprising. In a somewhat pater-
nalistic manner, he placed the terracing of the campus in the
hands of his railroad engineer, a Major Brooks.[47] Houck
laid plans for a double driveway to the school and furnished
trees that were planted along the walk of one of the main
streets leading to the institution. To insure protection of the
beauty of the campus, the presiding regent purchased and
donated ten acres of ground adjacent to its natural setting.
Out of remnants of rock and brick on this property, and
without special appropriation, the governing board erected a
house for the superintendent of the grounds. The stone used
in construction of the Education Building was a Houck
donation;[48] he gave seven acres of land to the normal school
for an athletic field.[49] "In all these improvements," remembered Houck, "I took a personal interest and gave them as
much time as I could well afford seeing that the work was
carried on economically and in a certain sense made
aesthetically attractive."[50] A college president later testified
that Houck's influence had brought about, at less cost,
better buildings than those possessed by any other teachers
college in the state.[51]

As might have been expected of a man of affairs, Louis
Houck lavished other gifts upon the institution. The Gerber
collection of classical statuary, prominently featured at the
Louisiana Exposition in St. Louis in 1904, was purchased at
a reputed sum of $40,000 and bequeathed to the college.[52]
The Beckwith Collection, an assortment of several thousand
specimens of warfare and the chase, agricultural implements,
domestic and ceremonial utensils, and articles of personal
adornment of the ancient "Mound Builders," was secured
for the college through its board president's friendship with
Thomas Beckwith.[53] With provincial satisfaction it was
rumored that the Smithsonian Institution had desired the
collection.[54]

To secure the exhibit, the college regent performed
meritorious services which underscored his legal and historical
talents. In "voluminous and diffusive and confusive" correspondence with the Beckwith family, he assured them

that the normal school was a secure depository for the relics. "At any rate," he added privately, "if the school is wiped out, it will be long after the Beckwith heirs have disappeared from the face of the earth."[55]

To fulfill a stipulation governing the college's possession of the collection, the Missouri historian delivered the first annual address on archaeology at the institution. In the tribute to Thomas Beckwith, Louis Houck unconsciously portrayed his own interests: "However much we may be engrossed in business, we still must have time for pursuits that give a higher and a nobler tone to life."[56] Houck later edited a Beckwith manuscript[57] and enumerated the archaeological findings in his first *History of Missouri* volume.[58]

True to the principles of the self-made man, Houck insisted upon better administrative and business-like operation of the college. As president of the board, he missed very few meetings of the regents and religiously spent Friday of each week scrutinizing affairs of the school.[59] As its chief executive, Houck insisted on regularity at all board meetings, the presence of all its members, and full expression of their opinions.[60] That Houck had an interest in the minutest affairs of the college can be judged from a letter to the *Cape Girardeau Democrat* in which he protested a charge of $75 for the student body's use of the non-taxed city fair grounds for their athletic contests.[61] He also wrote a letter urging the city to support a seventy-five thousand dollar bond issue for a new court house at Jackson because Cape Girardeau would soon want county support of additional appropriations for the normal school.[62] In 1905 Houck asked for an injunction to restrain the local fair association from selling liquor, as the sale of intoxicants might demoralize students of the college.[63] The purchase of Poland China hogs by the agriculture department of the college was approved by Houck for two purposes: to demonstrate the importance of using only registered livestock, and to save money on garbage collection.[64]

Perhaps Houck's greatest contribution to the college's program of expansion was his overturning the attitude that the board should be economical with state appropriations.

"When I went to the board about 1885," Houck stated, "the former boards had actually saved out of these [past] appropriations $5,000!"[65] His policy foreshadowed deficit spending theories of later generations of school administrators. In a letter to Senator William J. Stone, dated January 28, 1914, Houck mentioned the possibility of state teachers colleges' securing agricultural appropriations equal to those voted the University of Missouri. Although Houck regretted omission of scientific agriculture courses within the college curriculum,[66] his request for money differed from the reasoning of the state university because:

> We here in Missouri have five Normal Schools that are teaching agriculture, and that are doing I think really more effective work in diffusing agricultural instruction among the farmers than is done at Columbia. The work at Columbia is highly valuable and prepares, you might say, agricultural experts. The work that is done in the Normal Schools diffuses a general knowledge of the principles of agriculture through the rural school teachers, and what is needed is that the agricultural knowledge that we already have be diffused rather than that new experiments be made.[67]

In his quest for larger appropriations for his normal school at Cape Girardeau, Houck was, of course, antagonistic toward sizable grants for the University of Missouri at Columbia.[68] He was critical of an editorial comparison in a metropolitan paper that stated "appropriating for the University is like buying cloth to make a suit of clothes for a growing boy. It costs a little more each year because the boy is a little bigger."[69] According to the dispatch, the University was giving more per dollar than any other institution in the West. Examples of university economy were the professors "working for $2,600 a year whose ability would enable them to draw from two to five times that amount in business or in a better paid profession."

Houck spoke out against this "flaming article in favor of giving the university all they want." In writing of the problem of professors and small salaries, Houck displayed not only his antagonism toward the state university, but also unconsciously underscored the fact that he had assumed the cost of his own research and travel himself:

> Show me a professor anywhere that will stay at a small salary when he can get a bigger one elsewhere. They are always ready to pull out for a better job, and the Missouri University professor is no exception to the rule. And I understand that some of the professors of Missouri University get leave of absence to travel in foreign countries, their salary goes on all the same. I wish you would try to find out about that.[70]

Although larger appropriations were not always forthcoming, Houck was credited with being sufficiently resourceful in continuing the college's physical growth. That this ingenuity might have been exercised at the expense of the instructional budget was undoubtedly a faculty conjecture. Failing to secure appropriations for dormitories, Houck, L. J. Albert, and M. E. Leming organized a dormitory construction company which built two housing units. According to Houck, "The buildings were rented to the school for enough money to pay the interest on the loans that had to be made in order to raise the cash to build and that was all that could possibly be collected out of rent."[71] Later, the state appropriated money for the purchase of the buildings. The stadium and field house were named for Houck after his death because in the absence of financial underwriting by the Missouri legislature, he had encouraged and approved of the plans for building them. When an old lime kiln and rock quarry were bought by the college authorities for the purpose of transforming them into an athletic ground, local individuals questioned the feasibility of the project and the financial acumen of the promoters. Houck was credited with saying to the skeptics: "Any man can build a railroad if he has the money, but it's another thing when he does it without any."[72] It seemed not too much to expect that a man who had forged ahead in railroad construction, in spite of failure to procure expected land bonuses, would not be deterred by the absence of appropriations from continuing physical improvements on a college campus.

In every institutional project undertaken by the versatile southeast Missourian, there occurred, sooner or later, at least one dramatic incident. Such an episode in the otherwise routine history of the college, during the period Houck exercised dominant position on the board, was the dismissal of the college president, Dr. W. S. Dearmont, and the dean, Professor W. W. Martin. This was accomplished in 1921, with full concurrence of the head regent.

The outcome of the 1920 state and national election provided the condition out of which the dismissals came. The Republicans were victorious; a majority appointed to the governing staff of the school professed that party's faith. To the victors evidently belonged the spoils of administrative positions in Missouri's educational institutions. The mayor of the city began with a series of charges that, during the last campaign, the president of the college and other members of the faculty had utilized chapel periods each week to indoctrinate students with the views of the Democratic party.[73]

Dean W. W. Martin delivered a defiant speech to the new board, which only underscored political motivation. After stating that he had always been a Democrat and was still strongly in favor of the League of Nations, Martin significantly added: "Those who know me know that I never hide behind the skirts of my wife and in passing on my case I ask the board to judge me by my own course and not because my wife took an interest in the campaign."[74] He referred to Mrs. Martin, an ardent supporter of women's suffrage, because she had attracted a great deal of attention in a conservative community.[75] Mrs. Martin was given credit for unseating Senator James A. Reed of Missouri at the Democratic National Convention in San Francisco during the summer before. The "most publicized woman at the convention" had accomplished this feat by a speech which highlighted Reed's stand against the League of Nations and his personal hostility toward Wilson.[76]

When the board unanimously ousted Dr. Dearmont in June, 1921, the crusading St. Louis Post-Dispatch commented:

The League of Nations may boast another martyr and the victors of last November's election a fresh killing. Dr. W. S. Dearmont, late president of Cape Girardeau Teachers College entertained dangerous views. He was for the League of Nations and became "perniciously active" in its support. He even permitted friendly things to be said of it in the classroom. In other words, he allowed enthusiasm for world peace and international organization to blind his eyes to the expediency of maintaining peace and concord with all political elements upon whom he might become dependent for his job. . . .

The official head has been severed at the neck, and the League of Nations apostasy has been extracted, root and branch, from the Cape Girardeau institution.[77]

Pulitzer's paper further reasoned that if Missouri Republicans were permitted control of all colleges and universities in the country, all presidential incumbents would face dismissal, "for we have heard of no college president whose independent reasoning has not brought him to the support of the League." The *Illmo Jimplicute* penned a bitter news release:

Dr. Dearmont was removed from the presidency of the Teachers College this week and a man named Serena of Fulton elected in his stead. It is also reported that Dr. Sourbeer and Professor Sourkrout will also be elected members of the faculty.[78]

A Republican editor of southeast Missouri, who was later president of the board of curators of the University of Missouri, defended Dr. Dearmont for never intruding upon honest political opinion. Recalling that the college president had worked unceasingly for years to protect the young men and women from the saloon influences of the Cape, and that he had been active in local option and prohibition movements, Wolpers suggested that "in these fights with the Republicans in power in the Cape, he trampled on the toes of some of the leaders of the party but did so from a moral impulse and not from one of partisan politics."[79]

As Louis Houck, a Democrat, and best known member of the board, had cast his vote for the Dearmont dismissal, the question of motivation naturally arose. It was known that Houck, who was of German descent, was an opponent of both the League of Nations and the peace policies of Woodrow Wilson, and was a close personal friend of Senator Reed who championed identical viewpoints.[80] Then, too, Houck was a bitter critic of the Little River Drainage organization in southeast Missouri. As the Oliver family of lawyers represented the drainage district, and the Dearmonts and Olivers had family bonds, Houck's vote effectively registered his disapproval of this clan's growing influence in southeast Missouri affairs.[81]

The *Cape Girardeau Morning Sun* attributed dismissals to Dearmont's quarrel with Houck over teachers' salaries.[82] The *Sun* identified Dearmont as one who favored faculty salary increases in order to maintain proper standards of scholarship within the institution. The paper noted that a twenty per cent raise in salaries voted by the board had been delayed because of Houck's failure to make proper requisition, and then, when the increase was grudgingly granted, it had been made retroactive only to the first of the calendar year.

Despite Houck's stand on the Dearmont dismissal, the college has always seen fit to honor its long-term regent as its greatest benefactor. Its stadium and field house were named for him in 1930, during Republican years; the college's seventy-fifth anniversary homecoming event in 1949, during Democratic years, was in his honor.[83]

In 1902, the year of the successful sale of the St. Louis and Gulf to the St. Louis-San Francisco interests, Mr. and Mrs. Louis Houck announced their desire to give a public library to Cape Girardeau.[84] An expenditure of $30,000, which would provide a building, equipment, and books, was announced. The donors' only requirement was that the library should continue to be supported by a tax of two mills on the dollar upon all taxable property within the city.

When the library proposition was submitted to the voters, some opposition evidently manifested itself. The *Cape*

Girardeau Democrat cautioned that if the people spurned such cultural opportunity, rejection might endanger chances of obtaining a $250,000 appropriation for a new normal school structure to replace the recently burned college building.[85] Such an interpretation at least had the merit of aligning two of Houck's institutional interests. Perhaps such an argument was responsible for the acceptance of the library by the comfortable margin registered on October 4, 1902: 877, affirmative; 316, negative.[86]

Following public endorsement, Louis Houck disclosed his plans for the library building. His construction timetable envisioned putting in the foundation by late 1902 and completing the superstructure by the early summer of 1903. Such philanthropy corresponded in rough outline to the beneficence of another library donor, Andrew Carnegie, and Houck's explanations for building supplemented the self-help theories of the Gilded Age. In reasoning which foreshadowed his explanations for writing state and territorial histories, Houck urged upon his fellow citizens a library, "so that when the World's Fair opens in St. Louis and thousands of strangers are expected to come down the river and perhaps visit our city, we might not be ashamed of what we have here in the way of public institutions."[87]

Reminiscent of his legal episodes in railroad construction, Houck's offer of a library caused litigation extending from the Cape Girardeau circuit court to Missouri's highest tribunal.[88] The Supreme Court reversed the circuit court's decision that the city could accept the endowment. As Cape Girardeans had already imposed the maximum tax of fifty cents on the hundred dollars for general revenue purposes permitted by the state constitution for cities of third class, the justices ruled that the city could not collect an additional two-mill tax levy. The court added that the legislature could not grant the power to exceed the maximum rate, and that city authorities could not interpret a public library as a public school in order to secure the right to levy additional taxes. Hoping for a constitutional amendment, Houck deposited with the St. Louis Union Trust Company, for a five year period, $30,000 in St. Louis and Gulf bonds bearing four per cent interest.[89] The amendment was never realized. Thus the college remained the chief beneficiary of Houck's philanthropic impulses.

NOTES TO CHAPTER V

[1] *Journal of the House of Representatives of the 33rd General Assembly of Missouri* (Jefferson City, Missouri, 1885), pp. 40-41.

[2] *State Journal* (Jefferson City, Missouri), February 20, 1885.

[3] *Journal of the House of Representatives,* pp. 561-2; 1344.

[4] *Laws of the State of Missouri of the 33rd General Assembly* (Jefferson City, Missouri, 1885), pp. 210-2.

[5] *Official Directory of Missouri* (1885), p. 153.

[6] Houck, "Reminiscences" [Cape Girardeau, Missouri, n.d.], p. 223.

[7] *Report of Committee on charges against Honorable John Walker, State Auditor, together with the testimony of witnesses, 34th General Assembly of the state of Missouri* (Jefferson City, 1887), p. 175.

[8] *State Journal* (Jefferson City, Missouri), May 15, 1885.

[9] "Houck, "Reminiscences," p. 225.

[10] *La Grange Democrat,* La Grange, Missouri, [n.d.], reprinted in the *State Journal* (Jefferson City, Missouri), June 19, 1885, and the *St. Louis Post-Dispatch,* June 15, 1885.

[11] *St. Louis Post-Dispatch,* June 19, 1885.

[12] *Moberly Headlight* (Moberly, Missouri), [n.d.], reprinted in the *State Journal,* June 19, 1885.

[13] *State Journal,* June 19, 1885.

[14] *St. Louis Post-Dispatch,* June 13, 1885. Houck, of course, had made arrangements with the Anchor Line so that his Cape Girardeau railroad would become a "through route." See *17th Annual Report of the Railroad and Warehouse Commissioners of Missouri* (Jefferson City, Missouri, 1891), p. 121. Griff Prather was interested in the Anchor Line, but was best known as a member of the national committee of the Democratic Party.

[15] *St. Louis Post-Dispatch,* June 16, 1885. The earliest Cape Girardeau paper available is the *Cape Girardeau Democrat* in the year 1891. L. J. Albert's letter therefore represented one of the few rebuttals from a Girardean available besides Houck's testimony before the Walker investigating committee in 1887. See also *St. Louis Post-Dispatch,* June 17, 1885, for establishment of business relationship between Albert and Houck.

[16] *Moberly Headlight*, [n.d.], reprinted in *St. Louis Post Dispatch*, June 18, 1885.

[17] *Fredericktown Standard* (Fredericktown, Missouri), [n.d.], reprinted in *St. Louis Post Dispatch*, June 22, 1885.

[18] *St. Louis Post-Dispatch*, June 29, 1885.

[19] See *St. Louis Chronicle*, [n.d.], reprinted in *State Journal*, July 17, 1885; *Moberly Monitor*, reprinted in *St. Louis Post Dispatch*, July 10, 1885.

[20] *St. Louis Post-Dispatch*, June 19, 1885.

[21] *Report of the committee on charges against Honorable John Walker*, pp. 175-88.

[22] Houck, "Reminiscences," p. 227. He philosophically concluded: "Can it be that the necessary $5,000 was not forthcoming at other places, any more than at Cape Girardeau. . . . But it is evident from all this that sometimes it is a mistake not to pay the price demanded by people that under cover hold the winning hand." "Reminiscences," p. 228.

[23] *State Journal*, July 17, 1885.

[24] That selection of Cape Girardeau would be of benefit to St. Louis had been suggested by the *Missouri Republican* (St. Louis, Missouri), June 18 and July 9, 1885. On June 12, 1885, the *St. Louis Post-Dispatch* criticized the *Kansas City Times* for failing to note the superiority of the Cape Girardeau location. Only one special consideration did the *Post* grant to Kansas City: the supply of convicts furnished by that city to the state.

[25] *St. Louis Post-Dispatch*, July 8, 1885.

[26] *State Journal*, July 31, August 21, and September 4, 1885.

[27] *State Journal*, October 2, 1885.

[28] *Moberly Monitor* (Moberly, Missouri), [n.d.], reprinted in *St. Louis Post-Dispatch*, July 10, 1885.

[29] *State Journal*, September 4, 1884.

[30] *St. Louis Post-Dispatch*, June 13, June 18, 1885; March 15, 1887; *Missouri Republican*, June 18, 1885; March 15, 1887.

[31] *Missouri Republican*, March 29, and June 2, 1887.

[32] *Journal of the House of Representatives of the 34th General Assembly of the state of Missouri* (Jefferson City, 1887), p. 105. Charges were (1) that Walker, in consideration of the appointment of Charles A. Pollock as clerk in the state auditor's office, required Pollock to pay Walker $50 a month; (2) that Walker required Jas. A. Turner, late secretary of the State Board of Equalization, to pay Walker $175 so that Walker's son could have a horse, saddle, and bridle; (3) that Walker endeavored to secure D. H. McIntyre as special counsel in the "Hannibal and St. Joe" case for the consideration that McIntyre would purchase Walker's house; (4) that Walker purchased an interest in the Standard Boot and Shoe Company, a company engaged in working convict labor; (5) that Louis Houck and others paid Walker $2,000 for his Cape Girardeau vote in location of the branch penitentiary.

[33] *Report of the Committee on charges against Honorable John Walker,* p. 178. Also see *Missouri Republican,* March 15, 1887.

[34] *Missouri Republican,* March 29, 1887.

[35] *St. Louis Post-Dispatch,* March 15, 1887.

[36] *Missouri Republican,* March 29, 1887.

[37] *Laws of the state of Missouri of the 34th General Assembly,* Jefferson City, Missouri, 1887, p. 227.

[38] *Journal of the Senate of the 34th General Assembly of Missouri* (Jefferson City, 1887), p. 137; *Journal of the House of Representatives* (Jefferson City, 1887), p. 200. Whitelaw was a Cape Girardean who helped prepare a bill which provided that two-thirds of the amounts collected on the saloon licenses of the city be applied to the payment of interest on the railroad bonds subscribed by the city. Madison R. Smith was one of the principal Houck lawyers during the famous controversies with the Gould railroad interests.

[39] *Southeast Missouri State College Homecoming Bulletin* (Cape Girardeau, Missouri, October 14-15, 1949).

[40] Houck was a member of the Board of Regents from June 3, 1886, to February 17, 1925; secretary of the Board of Regents from June 19, 1886, to June 5, 1889; member of the executive committee of the board from June 18, 1886, to February 17, 1925; and president of the Board of Regents from June 5, 1889, to February 17, 1925. *Cape Girardeau News,* October 20, 1949. *Also see* Floyd Shoemaker, *The Messages and Proclamations of the Governors of the State of Missouri,* XII (1930), 263 and 359.

[41] R. S. Douglass, "History of the Missouri State Normal School at Cape Girardeau," *Educational Outlook,* Cape Girardeau, Missouri, 1913-14. Consult following issues: I, No. 1, 20-24; I, No. 3, 114-7; I, No. 4, 214-6; II, No. 2, 58-61; II, No. 3, 158-64. Also see *Weekly Republican* (Cape Girardeau, Missouri), June 7, 1912.

[42] Houck, "Reminiscences," pp. 197 ff.

[43] *Missouri Republican,* December 18, 1874.

[44] Houck, "Reminiscences," p. 203.

[45] Mark Twain, *Life on the Mississippi* (New York, 1883), p. 151.

[46] *Cape Girardeau News,* October 20, 1949.

[47] Houck, "Reminiscences," p. 210 ff.

[48] *The Capaha Arrow,* Southeast Missouri State College, Cape Girardeau, Missouri, October 19, 1949.

[49] *Daily Republican* (Cape Girardeau, Missouri), May 25, 1905.

[50] Houck, "Reminiscences," p. 223.

[51] *Cape Girardeau Southeast Missourian,* February 19, 1925.

52 *Daily Republican,* June 19, 1905.

53 See following articles regarding Beckwith Collection and the career of Thomas Beckwith of Charleston, Missouri, in the *Weekly Republican* (Cape Girardeau, Missouri), June 23, 1911; October 23 and 30, 1914.

54 *Cape Girardeau Southeast Missourian,* February 18, 1925.

55 Letter to Edward A. Rozier, Farmington, Missouri, [n.d.], Louis Houck's miscellaneous correspondence, president's office, Southeast Missouri State College, Cape Girardeau, Missouri.

56 The address, "Thomas Beckwith: Farmer-Archaeologist," was published in the *Educational Outlook,* II (Cape Girardeau, Missouri, 1914-15), 113-22.

57 Louis Houck editor, Thomas Beckwith, "The Story of the Settlement and Settlers of Mississippi County, Missouri," Kent Library, Southeast Missouri State College, Cape Girardeau, Missouri. Houck's preface dated November 24, 1917.

58 Louis Houck, *History of Missouri,* I (Chicago, 1908), 60-4.

59 *Cape Girardeau Southeast Missourian,* January 31, 1919.

60 *Ibid.*

61 *Cape Girardeau Democrat,* November 14, 1893.

62 *Weekly Republican,* August 25, 1905.

63 *Daily Republican,* October 9, 1905.

64 *Southeast Missourian* (Cape Girardeau, Missouri), March 19, 1949.

65 Houck, "Reminiscences," p. 210.

66 *Missouri Historical Review,* XXXV, No. 1 (October, 1940), 82-3. Also see *St. Louis Republic,* August 6, 1911, concerning preparation of agricultural students at the Cape Girardeau college.

67 Letter to Senator William J. Stone, January 28, 1914. In a letter to Representative J. J. Russell, January 28, 1914, Houck requested federal aid for agricultural work at the normal schools of the state. Louis Houck's miscellaneous correspondence, president's office, Southeast Missouri State College, Cape Girardeau, Missouri.

68 See Jonas Viles, *The University of Missouri, A Centennial History* (Columbia, Missouri, 1939), p. 34, for indications of enmity between teachers colleges and the state university.

69 *St. Louis Republic,* January 19, 1915.

70 Letter to Representative H. W. Bridges, January 20, 1915. Louis Houck's miscellaneous correspondence, president's office, Southeast Missouri State College, Cape Girardeau, Missouri.

71 Houck, "Reminiscences," p. 214.

[72] *Southeast Missourian,* March 19, 1949.

[73] *Cape Girardeau Southeast Missourian,* June 6, 1921.

[74] *Ibid.,* June 8, 1921.

[75] *Ibid.,* August 14, 1914. Also see Mrs. W. W. Martin, "Equal Suffrage and Social Welfare," *Educational Outlook,* II, No. 4 (Cape Girardeau, Missouri, 1915), 224-36.

[76] William G. Shepherd, "Mrs. Martin 'got' Jim Reed" (International News Service feature story), *Cape Girardeau Southeast Missourian,* June 30, 1920.

[77] *St. Louis Post-Dispatch* editorial, reprinted in *Cape Girardeau Morning Sun,* June 11, 1921.

[78] *Illmo Jimplicute* (Illmo, Missouri), editorial, reprinted in *Cape Girardeau Morning Sun,* June 12, 1921.

[79] *Cape Girardeau Morning Sun,* April 2, 1921.

[80] *Cape Girardeau Southeast Missourian,* April 22, 1925.

[81] Russell L. Dearmont, son of Dr. W. S. Dearmont, had married the only daughter of Mr. and Mrs. R. B. Oliver. R. B. Oliver had once been a Houck lawyer. In 1932 Russell Dearmont ran as a Democratic candidate for governor of Missouri; in 1957 he became president of the Missouri Pacific, former Gould property in conflict with Houck railroad interests. The Oliver family has been closely affiliated with the University of Missouri; several of them served as members of the boards of curators. Russell Dearmont has become a regent of the state college at Cape Girardeau in recent years.

[82] *Cape Girardeau Sun,* June 9, 1921. The two Cape newspapers at this time reflected the Houck and Oliver interests. The *Cape Girardeau Southeast Missourian,* a Republican paper, favored Houck; the *Cape Girardeau Sun,* a Democratic paper, was edited by Charles C. Oliver. See editorial in *Cape Girardeau Southeast Missourian,* May 23, 1919, relating to interests backing the *Sun.*

[83] *Southeast Missouri State College Homecoming Bulletin* (Cape Girardeau, Missouri, October 14-15, 1949).

[84] *Cape Girardeau Democrat,* August 2, 1902.

[85] *Ibid.,* September 27, 1902.

[86] Cape Girardeau's acceptance was in accordance with section 6466, *Revised Statutes of Missouri,* 1899, amended by an act of March 9, 1901. See *Laws of the state of Missouri of the 41st General Assembly,* 1901 (Jefferson City, Missouri, 1901), p. 84.

[87] *Cape Girardeau Democrat,* November 22, 1902.

[88] "Brooks, Appellant, vs. Schultz, Collector," *Missouri Reports,* CLXXVIII (Columbia, Missouri, 1904), pp. 222-8.

[89] *Cape Girardeau Democrat,* April 23, 1904. In later years, when Cape Girardeau was contemplating a Carnegie Library, Houck intimated he would offer free acreage for the building site. *Cape Girardeau Morning Sun,* June 16, 1911.

CHAPTER VI

ACT OF FAITH AND FRAME OF REFERENCE: THE MAKING OF A STATE HISTORIAN

"During a somewhat busy and active life, by no means devoted to literary pursuits, the interesting material embodied in this work has been collected. For me it has been a labor of love, absorbing for a long time nearly all my leisure hours — diverting my mind from business cares."—Louis Houck, *A History of Missouri* (Chicago, 1908), I, v.

LOUIS HOUCK, Missouri's "Foremost Historian,"[1] did not belong to the majority in the profession for whom history was ever a bread and butter question. Rather did he fit into the exceptional class, one of the few who had been financially lucky because of parents and wife. Like James Ford Rhodes he had, in addition to inherited comfortable circumstances, created his own affluent condition which enabled the historian "in the afternoon of [his] days to approach Clio without mercenary impulses."[2]

However, Louis Houck was not a James Ford Rhodes, either in political sentiment or productivity. He did not one day, to the exclusion of business cares, shut the door of his office and open that of his library, as purportedly did Rhodes. The Missouri writer collected his research materials during a vexatious business career. Simultaneously with this career, he created sufficient leisure in which to edit and interpret historical data, a stimulating process which helped divert his mind from troublesome railroad interests. Thus Houck could never have agreed with another transportation enthusiast, Henry Ford, that "history was the bunk." Rather was he to be compared with his contemporary, Jay Gould, his business mentor, who had also discovered historical pursuits to be an interesting and sometimes necessary diversion.[3]

94

In 1901, at the age of sixty-one, Louis Houck actively resumed his erudite interests with publication of *The Boundaries of the Louisiana Purchase.*[4] This historical work, legal and argumentative in nature, reflected the manifest destiny of the era by depositing all of Montana, Idaho, Oregon, and Washington in the galaxy of the Louisiana Purchase states. Inasmuch as its purpose was to magnify and idealize celebration of the centenary of the Louisiana Purchase, *The American Historical Review* gave it scant notice.[5] More significant than its curt reception, however, was that the work was preliminary to Houck's major opus, *A History of Missouri*, which appeared in 1908 when Houck was almost seventy years of age. The three volume, 1200 page study of the early territorial and colonial history of the state and its companion two volumes of documents entitled *The Spanish Regime in Missouri*, published in 1909, became the basis of Houck's historical fame in Missouri.[6]

Certain factors accounted for the success of "Houck's History," as it was familiarly called. Reviews immediately made it the "sacred cow" of Missouri historiography.

Jonas Viles, chairman of the history department of the University of Missouri, in an analysis of Houck's work for *The American Historical Review*, was favorably disposed. He heralded the appearance of a "comprehensive history of Missouri" for all interested students of the history of the West. Professor Viles commented:

> The history is clearly written and despite the mass of factual information is redeemed from dullness by the enthusiasm, and, especially in the later chapters, by the shrewd common-sense of the writer. But unless one is familiar with the unorganized condition of the materials and the lack of preliminary studies, he cannot appreciate the difficulties of the subject, nor how successfully, on the whole, Mr. Houck has surmounted them.[7]

When the Missouri Historical Society of St. Louis was informed that the history was soon to be issued from the press, it set the critical tone of Missouri's learned societies and learned men with an advance notice:

For excellence in its execution, as well as for intrinsic interest, the work will easily hold the front rank among state histories. Since it reaches only to the admission of Missouri to the Union, it is greatly hoped that Mr. Houck will supplement it with a volume giving an account of the people and events of his own time.[8]

Several years later the Society expanded its remarks:

. . . it covers the period of the beginnings of our history so thoroughly that the story of that time will never have to be rewritten. And it sets the standard so high that we may confidently hope that future writers who continue the work down to our own times may be encouraged to maintain an equal level.[9]

This aura of definitiveness surrounding Houck's history confronted Floyd C. Shoemaker, assistant librarian and later secretary of the State Historical Society of Missouri, Columbia, Missouri, when in 1913 he was engaged in gathering biographical material on the fathers of the Missouri constitution. A letter from "A Reader" in the *St. Louis Republic* intimated that Shoemaker was wasting his time, as all important data needed by the secretary was contained in Houck's history. After all, Houck had procured with difficulty the reliable facts and had estimated correctly all missing details of local history and genealogy. For good measure, the "Reader" added:

And right here it is not inopportune to say that Houck's *History of Missouri*, colonial and territorial, is a performance of rare merit and in my humble opinion a work that ought to be in every public library of the State, and as for that in the library of every Missourian taking an interest in its history.[10]

The State Historical Society secretary, who had gathered twice the amount of material Houck had compiled, nevertheless acknowledged by his reply Houck's position in Missouri historiography:

No student of Missouri history appreciates more fully the invaluable character of his great work than the present writer. It is undoubtedly the greatest compilation of facts relating to the early history of this State that exists today and is a veritable encyclopedia in that line. It has proven a mine of information to both the student and man of affairs and is especially strong in the field of biography. No student of history, and especially of Missouri history, can be too complimentary in his expression of appreciation of Mr. Houck's *History of Missouri* and there is no praise that would be too generous to bestow on the author. The State of Missouri is to be congratulated upon having so public spirited a man who is both willing and able to undertake and complete in so satisfactory a manner the early history of this commonwealth. The cost of interpreting the French and Spanish documents of this State and the immense labor of compiling this history should make every Missourian feel deeply indebted to this wonderful man.[11]

The officialdom of Missouri historical organizations saw fit to honor Houck, and he, in turn, served in official capacities for the state societies. As a member of the advisory committee of the Missouri Historical Society, Houck promised the organization a part of his documentary collection. In 1901 he was elected an honorary member of the society.[12] In connection with the State Historical Society of Missouri, Louis Houck accepted trusteeship, serving two periods, 1901-1904, and 1914-1925, and also acted as second vice-president of the society from 1916 to 1925.[13]

Another factor in Houck's historical success was that he foreshadowed developments in the writing of state history related to research materials and scholarly assistance. Houck himself realized that the early territorial period of Missouri history had not been published. In order to translate his setting accurately, he utilized foreign documents, archaeological surveys, local county records, as well as contemporary travel accounts and reminiscences. Wise enough to admit that he was not the master of all types of problems, he accepted expert assistance. From the standpoint of the history guild, his employment of James Alexander Robertson and Idress Head [later Mrs. Clarence W. Alvord] was perhaps the most significant.[14] Don José Gonzales Verger ferreted from the Archives of the Indies at Seville the necessary documents. Quite freely, Louis Houck expressed his indebtedness to Walter B. Douglass, Marie Louise Dalton, Pierre Chouteau, and William Beers.[15]

That Houck's production was "a labor of love" contributed to its favorable reception; there were many passages of eloquent testimony of affection for the territorial features of old Missouri.[16] If these sparked readers' interest, it perhaps indicated that Louis Houck was to some degree a Francis Parkman who encompassed the territory of his subject. Samuel Eliot Morison recently charged:

> You can count on the fingers of one hand the American historians now writing who can describe a scene, an event, or a natural setting in such a way that the reader can see it. (The reason is largely that the writer cannot see it himself; he sits in a library and writes instead of going about by whatever means of transportation is available, and finding out for himself what historic sites look like today.)[17]

By virtue of his railroad surveying and construction in the state in the last half of the nineteenth century, Louis Houck escaped such censure. He had traversed Missouri terrain and he appreciated pioneer endeavors.

Houck's pre-eminence in the Missouri history field can also be explained by the copyright dates of his major works, 1908 and 1909. He probably could not have subsidized publication sooner because it was not until his sale of the St. Louis and Gulf system to the St. Louis-San Francisco railroad interests in 1902 that he felt financially secure. If he had published much later, he would have encountered a period in which history had been transformed from a literary avocation into a highly professionalized discipline. Scholars estimate that by 1910 history was "universally recognized as a research discipline as rigorous and exacting—if not quite so exact in its conclusions—as any university study not mathematical in its methods."[18] In a chronological sense, the period was as perfect a time for Louis Houck to compose

Missouri history as it once had been for him to assume the role of a railroad builder who had "a penchant for gathering rails —some old, some new, not very heavy—and making a railroad out of them."[19]

For Houck's generation, the chief values of his histories were the encyclopedic rendition of facts plus flattering biographical sketches of early residents. For several years his works were cited in scholars' bibliographies and footnote references,[20] though their primary use was for the identification of persons who played minor roles in Missouri territorial history. As the next generation of state historians de-emphasized biographical detail, reappraisal of Houck's writings suggests the form of criticism once leveled at Reuben Gold Thwaites, also a territorial historian. As Clarence W. Alvord characterized Thwaites, so might one suggest of Houck: "Trained in business and the newspaper profession his mind was that of the entrepreneur, to whom the slow, laborious process of monographic writing made no appeal."[21]

In a comment on Thwaites, not inapplicable to Houck, the iconoclastic Alvord said:

> [Thwaites'] mind was trained for the examination of details, for an appreciation of the fringes of the garment rather than the garment itself; it is the description of the fringe which the great public, that he courted all his life, loves to hear described. In his written work it is seldom that we are able to find a real appreciation of the hidden motives of men or of the great underlying forces of which events perceptible to the senses are but the results. Even his fondness for detail did not mean correctness of detail; nor would this be expected of one who never produced monographic studies.

As Mrs. Alvord once implied, when asked to compare the territorial historians, Louis Houck and Clarence W. Alvord, that the Illinois professor spent long hours upon historical composition, while the Missouri chronicler proceeded more swiftly in his literary efforts.[22]

The response to Houck's work by the public he may have courted was both complimentary and revealing. Local newspapers were pleased that "Houck's History" restored southeast Missouri to its rightful position in the history of the state. As one editor implied, the foundations of the great Missouri commonwealth were laid in the state's bootheel.[23] Even the metropolitan papers, in their compliments to Houck, reflected a midwestern sectional bias:

> New England owes her tremendous hold upon the thought and imagination of all Americans primarily, of course, to the exceptional men she has contributed to the nation's life; but their influence has been greatly extended and intensified by the fact that in that barren region with its inhospitable climate writers spring indigenous to the soil. The rest of the nation has looked at American history through New England's eyes. Missouri has been rich in notable men, but has yet to raise up an adequate plentiful crop of writers to render their virtues and achievements illustrious. All the more ought we to honor such labors as Mr. Houck's. His meaty volumes will be a rich storehouse for the future teller of Missouri tales and the historian of particular periods. And this honor should be rendered while the author is yet with us. All worthy work is fairly certain of ultimate recognition. The real test of the greatness of a people's heart and mind is contemporary recognition of those whose labors "do the State some service."[24]

A few mildly criticized Houck's history. Professor Viles felt compelled to note certain faults incident to the lack of special training frankly confessed by the author: sources of information, especially in biographical details, were not always clear despite numerous footnotes and references; there was lack of uniformity in the citation of titles; and no list of authorities was available at the conclusion of the work.[25] Professor Isaac Joslin Cox, of the University of Cincinnati, complained of the unfortunate method of publishing translations of source material without originals. In Houck's *Spanish Regime*, Cox found it somewhat disconcerting that Houck's translator, Dr. J. A. Robertson, questioned the accuracy of transcripts.[26] Arrangement of documents, partly chronological and partly topical, was confusing to the critic. Complaint was registered over the lack of uniformity and consistency in descriptive headings.

These were but little-noticed criticisms buried in professional historical journals. To most Missourians the endeavors of Louis Houck were praiseworthy because they were accomplished with philanthropic fervor. Since "none but an author of the public spirit and wealth of Honorable Louis Houck would have attempted [a state history] and despite a well-ascertained future loss have succeeded,"[27] it was thought necessary to reckon the cost. This was calculated at $100,000.[28] In the manner of a patron, Houck disclaimed any hope of retrieving the investment. When the books did not sell widely, Houck offered to dispose of remaining sets at a reduced price, "as it was never his intention to make a commercial proposition of his labors."[29] Perhaps as a result of their failure to sell, or flushed by enthusiasm for Missouri's centennial celebration, Houck made a gift of his histories to every first-class high school in the state.[30] However, the newspaper firm which in later years agreed to dispose of the remaining volumes, never disavowed a commercial interest in the books. Since editions were limited, broad hints were dropped that purchase might prove to be a profitable investment.[31] Earlier, readers had been advised that since sales were restricted, "the opportunity to acquire [the histories] when they become of tremendous value will be impossible."[32]

Despite the fact that Houck had achieved marked success as a state historian, he did not honor the request of the Missouri Historical Society to continue his history beyond the date of Missouri's admission to statehood. Although his advanced age may have accounted for this, his last fifteen years of life were filled with smaller historical projects. In 1915 was published Louis Houck's *Memorial Sketches of Pioneers and Early Residents of Southeast Missouri.* For private distribution, Houck had recorded

> the life story of dear and loved personal friends, unknown to the wide and tumultous world, and who quietly after a life of usefulness went to the realms

beyond. Their memory is dear to me and fondly I
hope, for a little time at least, to preserve their
honored names and virtues in these pages.[33]

One reviewer observed that

> while the memorials have no particular literary
> value, they present in clear and simple language the
> salient characteristics and the most important events
> in the lives of their subjects, and they thus consti-
> tute an important addition to the store of tradition
> of southeast Missouri.[34]

The Missouri Historical Review believed it noteworthy that
Louis Houck had seen fit to include three women in his group
of twelve pioneers since it was not customary to portray
the role of women in the development of state history.[35]

In 1917 Louis Houck edited Thomas Beckwith's "The
Story of the Settlement and Settlers of Mississippi County,
Missouri."[36] He continued similar assistance to other local
historians.[37] In numerous speeches before city organizations,
he employed historical themes. By virtue of his combined
interest in railroad building and history, Houck designated
historical titles for villages and towns in southeast Missouri.[38]

Just twice did Houck explain his compulsion for writing
history; to a newspaper reporter he admitted:

> Many men desire nothing better for a monument to
> their memory than an ornate headstone at the head
> of their last resting place. I believe this early his-
> tory of Missouri, where I and my family have resided
> so long, will live longer in the minds of the living
> than any gravestone that I might provide for in my
> last will or which may be erected to my memory
> by my family.[39]

In his memoirs he confessed:

> During my life I always took a great interest in the
> growth and development of the country in which I
> lived but also in its history generally. In me it was
> so to speak, a compelling instinct. It was impossible
> for me to live in a country and become identified
> in its business or its people living in it without tak-

ing an interest in its early settlement and growth and the development of its agricultural, industrial, and social life.[40]

He had indeed written history "as a sideline [which would] serve to integrate the historian with his community, to make him a valued and respected member of it, instead of 'just another professor' [or entrepreneur]."[41]

NOTES TO CHAPTER VI

[1] *St. Louis Post-Dispatch,* March 1, 1925; *Missouri Historical Review,* XIX (1925), 475-6.

[2] Conyers Read, "The Social Responsibilities of the Historian," *American Historical Review,* LV (January, 1950), 276.

[3] Allen Nevins, "Jay Gould," *Dictionary of American Biography,* ed. Allen Johnson and Dumas Malone, VII (New York, 1936), 454-5.

[4] Louis Houck, *The Boundaries of the Louisiana Purchase* (St. Louis, 1901).

[5] Frederick W. Moore, *American Historical Review,* VII (1902), 608.

[6] Louis Houck, *A History of Missouri* (3 vols.; Chicago, 1908); *The Spanish Regime in Missouri* (2 vols.; Chicago, 1909); favorable estimate by Dixon Ryan Fox, "State History—I," *Political Science Quarterly,* XXXVI (1921), 578.

[7] *American Historical Review,* XIV (1909), 834-5.

[8] *Missouri Historical Society Collections,* III (1908), 98.

[9] *Ibid.* (1911), p. 313.

[10] *St. Louis Republic,* July 24, 1913.

[11] *Ibid.,* July 29, 1913.

[12] Maynard C. Willis, "Red Letter Books Relating to Missouri," *Missouri Historical Review,* XXXV (1940), 85; *St. Louis Republic,* May 10, 1908; *Yearbook of the Missouri Historical Society* (St. Louis, 1926), p. 161.

[13] Floyd C. Shoemaker, *A History of the State Historical Society of Missouri, 1898-1948* (Columbia, Missouri, 1948), pp. 9, 28, 146.

[14] James Alexander Robertson was a graduate of Western Reserve University, specializing in Romance languages. From 1896 Robertson was engaged on Reuben Gold Thwaites' *The Jesuit Relations;* from

1900-1901, in Madison, Wisconsin, Robertson worked on a two-volume index for Thwaites' seventy-three volumes of *The Jesuit Relations.* Dr. Robertson spent the years 1902 to 1907 in archives and libraries of Spain, Portugal, France, Italy, England, and the United States. *See* A. Curtis Wilgus, "The Life of James Alexander Robertson," and "The Published Writings of James Alexander Robertson," A. Curtis Wilgus, editor, *Hispanic American Essays, A Memorial to James Alexander Robertson* (Chapel Hill, 1942), pp. 3-14, 15-30.

All documents published by Houck in *The Spanish Regime* were translated by Robertson, except for one item translated by Joseph Vaeth, faculty member of the State Normal College at Cape Girardeau.

Mrs. Alvord has told the writer that one of the first checks Louis Houck made before he employed her as a research assistant was to test her ability with the Romance languages. One evening Houck gave her some manuscripts to take home and translate. The next day he asked her to read the manuscripts for him, and evidently was pleased with her performance because she got the job the next day. Interview with Mrs. Alvord, Columbia, Missouri, fall, 1950.

[15] Douglas was the president of the Missouri Historical Society in 1903-4, and member of its advisory committee. Miss Dalton was the librarian of the Missouri Historical Society. Upon her death, Mrs. Alvord became librarian. See tribute paid to Miss Dalton by Louis Houck and Dr. C. W. Alvord in the *Missouri Historical Society Collections,* III (1908), 5. Chouteau, one of the descendants of the founders of St. Louis, placed at Houck's disposal some of his papers and also pictures illustrating the Spanish epoch of the history of the state of Missouri which Houck incorporated into his state history. William Beers was the distinguished librarian of the Howard Memorial Library of New Orleans, Louisiana.

[16] Louis Houck, *A History of Missouri,* I (Chicago, 1908), 31-32. Also see *St. Louis Star,* February 21, 1925.

[17] Samuel Eliot Morison, "Faith of a Historian," *The American Historical Review,* LVI (1951), 273.

[18] John Herman Randall, Jr., and George Haines, IV, "Controlling Assumptions in the Practice of American Historians," *Theory and Practice in Historical Study: A Report of the Committee on Historiography* (Social Science Research Council Bulletin No. 54, [New York, 1946], p. 24).

[19] Henry Wollman, "The Strange Story of the Cape Girardeau Railroad," *Commercial Law Journal,* XXXVIII (1933), 1.

[20] Clarence W. Alvord, James Alexander Robertson, Herbert E. Bolton and Thomas Maitland Marshall used Houck as references in their works. Houck is always included in any of the standard history textbooks, bibliographies, and encyclopedia articles written by Jonas Viles, Floyd C. Shoemaker, Perry Rader, and others.

[21] "A Critical Analysis of the Work of Reuben Gold Thwaites," *Proceedings of the Mississippi Valley Historical Association,* VII (Cedar Rapids, 1914), 325. This address shocked some, as Thwaites

had not been dead over seven months. See Marion Dargan, Jr., "Clarence Walworth Alvord," *Marcus W. Jernegan Essays in American Historiography,* ed. William T. Hutchinson (Chicago, 1937), p. 335.

[22] Interview, Mrs. Alvord, Columbia, Missouri, fall, 1950.

[23] *Weekly Republican* (Cape Girardeau, Missouri), June 26, 1908.

[24] *St. Louis Republic,* July 24, 1913.

[25] *The American Historical Review,* XIV (1909), 834-5.

[26] *The American Historical Review,* XVI (1910), 172-3.

[27] *Missouri Historical Review,* IX (1915), 266.

[28] *St. Louis Republic,* May 10, 1908.

[29] *Cape Girardeau Southeast Missourian,* January 24, 1919.

[30] Maynard C. Willis, "Red Letter Books Relating to Missouri," *Missouri Historical Review,* XXXV (1940), 86.

[31] *Weekly Republican,* December 4, 1908.

[32] *Daily Republican* (Cape Girardeau, Missouri), July 17, 1908.

[33] Louis Houck, *Memorial Sketches of Pioneers and Early Residents of Southeast Missouri* (Cape Girardeau, Missouri, 1915), p. i.

[34] E. M. Violette, in *The Mississippi Valley Historical Review,* III (1916), 417.

[35] *Missouri Historical Review,* X (1915), 46.

[36] "The Story of the Settlement and Settlers of Mississippi County, Missouri" (1917), unpublished manuscript, Kent Library, Cape Girardeau, Missouri. Also see Louis Houck, "Thomas Beckwith: The Farmer-Archaeologist," *Educational Outlook* (1914), pp. 113-22; Louis Houck, *A History of Missouri,* I (Chicago, 1908), 52, 60-64.

[37] Acknowledgment of indebtedness to Houck was made by Robert Sidney Douglass in his *History of Southeast Missouri,* I (Chicago, 1912), virtually *passim.* Also see C. F. Marbut, "The Evolution of the Northern Part of the Lowlands of Southeastern Missouri," *The University of Missouri Studies,* I (1902), ed. Frank Thilly (Columbia, Missouri, 1902), p. vi; and James Alexander Robertson, *Louisiana Under the Rule of Spain, France, and the United States,* I (Cleveland, 1911), 18, 23.

[38] *Cape Girardeau Democrat,* July 13, 1907; Mayme Lucille Hamlett, "Place Names of Six Southeast Counties of Missouri," (unpublished Master's thesis, University of Missouri, 1938), pp. 207-9, and *St. Louis Post Dispatch,* April 28, 1951.

[39] *St. Louis Republic,* May 10, 1908.

[40] Houck, "Reminiscences," p. 264.

[41] Samuel Eliot Morison, "Faith of a Historian," *The American Historical Review,* LVI (1951), 273.

Chapter VII

LOUIS HOUCK: MAN AND MYTH

"A little subconscious egotism is allowable as a trick of speech to a man who has achieved some greatness (not from things merely said, but) on the arduous plane of things actually done. It must be remembered that Mr. Houck was speaking of things not inaptly described by the phrase of the old worthy (Caesar, maybe): 'All of which I saw and much of which I was.' "—"The Donaldson Bond and Stock Company, vs. Louis Houck," *Missouri Reports*, CCXIII (Columbia, Missouri, July 3, 1909), 429.

Ɪɴ 1872 an unidentified observer penned a picture of young Louis Houck, recently arrived in the Missouri bootheel:

> Another of Southeast Missouri's promising men is Louis Houck of Cape Girardeau, but he is so modest in his pretensions that it can hardly be said that he is aspiring. I don't know when I met a man that impressed me more favorably than did Mr. Houck when I first made his acquaintance yesterday at Jackson where he is attending court. But he needs no commendation from me; his reputation as a lawyer is not confined to this state. Though small in physical organization, he is massive in intellect for one of his age. He is very affable, is a gentleman of culture and learning; he has a fine discriminating judgment and has evidently studied the science of government with attention.[1]

In later years, Louis Houck, by virtue of his victories over Jay Gould, could hardly be portrayed as modest.[2] In all other respects, however, he had more than lived up to early expectations that "from the appearance of the gentleman we take him to be a first class citizen and lawyer."[3]

106

After achievement of success in varied fields, perhaps he was entitled to expressions of intense individualism.

By profuse employment of the personal pronouns and adjectives, "I," "Mine," "My," and "Myself," Louis Houck amused (as well as confused) many a court of law in his legal skirmishes to retain control of numerous short-line railroad concerns. As a lawyer-railroad director, he not only utilized the fourteenth amendment in an unique consideration of the corporation as a person, and as such entitled to protection of its property rights from the encroachments of more powerful railroad consolidations, he also dramatically and ostentatiously identified himself with the companies he headed as one mistreated personality.[4] In an age of increasing transportation mergers, the legal profession was consistently served such anachronistic expressions of the Missouri entrepreneur as "my rates, my railroad, my depots, and my trains."[5] In the last quarter of the nineteenth century, Houck idioms must have afforded nostalgic diversion to men of an era who possibly considered themselves no longer masters of their economic fates, much less captains of their industrialized souls.[6]

In the reform year of 1887, an unwary state legislative committee, charged with the heavy responsibility of securing uniform passenger and freight rates for Missouri railroads, committed the tactical error of summoning the individualistic Louis Houck as a friendly witness. Being an advocate of free enterprise, he protested all regulation, whether it adversely affected himself or his more powerful rivals. While bitterly denouncing a proposed law equating his rates with those of his opponents, he made the delightful declaration in an outraged voice: "Why that would make myself and the Iron Mountain [Gould railroad property] one road."[7] Laughter brightened, although it ended, that day's work of the sober committee.

A Supreme Court justice, explicating a complex problem of personal or corporate ownership, stated sympathetically the best defense of Houck's "possessive predisposition." If a man had succeeded in his arduous struggle with adversity, he was entitled to egotistical phraseology. If he incorrectly linked his corporations to himself, he was to be likened to a Caesar who equated the times with his own person.[8]

Spotlighting for urban sophisticates the career of a man whose "life story would read like a romance," the *St. Louis Post-Dispatch* headlined a feature story: *By Louis Houck— A School, Six Books, 500 Miles of Railroad, Only Man Who Ever Beat Jay Gould in a Deal.*[9] To his business associates, however, Houck was more than a statistical enumeration of achievements. He was properly personalized as "a bundle of energy who tried to put some life into the old town of Cape Girardeau."[10] He was known as a privileged character who had dined on waffles with Jay Gould aboard the wizard's private railroad car. When Gould ate more of the pancakes than his doctors advised, Houck could report to his cohorts the robber baron's retort: "A man might as well be killed for stealing a sheep as a lamb."[11] And on occasion, Houck could also elevate Gould's reply to the status of a business maxim by portrayal of himself as the sacrificial lamb served up to the corporate forces of Wall Street.

Houck's office was more incongruous than Gould's. Located in the old Baptist Church of the city, it provided effective scenery for an Horatio Alger drama. When the local hero bested the age's well known railroad king in that setting, it was inevitable that Houck be teased by his fundamentalist brethren with the scriptural quotation: "My house shall be called a house of prayers, but you make it a den of thieves."[12] Thus, the morality play in praise of native ingenuity had achieved perfect staging.[13] Gaiety had brightened somber Main Street.

As a former journalist sufficiently wise in the ways of the press to adopt the strategy of identification of himself and his projects with the good of a section and a state, Houck was no doubt immensely pleased by the multiplying anecdotes. Accounts accented his rural Western-Southern traits of individualism, local shrewdness, scholarly absentmindedness, and economy made necessary by his shortage of capital.

Illustrative of late nineteenth century American attitudes were two favorite recollections about Houck. The nearsighted railroad executive, embarking on an inspection tour of recently laid track in virginal southeast Missouri, accidentally stepped on a big brush. As the branch flew up, tapping him on the shoulder, Houck quickened his step. Subconsciously revealing his persistent financial anxieties, he said brusquely to the unrecognized and unwanted intruder: "Yes, yes, Tom, I'll have the money for you tomorrow."[14]

Actually, such a tale was not too different from the one recounted by Houck in his memoirs. "No one would work for my railroad company," confided Houck, and "from the start I was annoyed by unreasonable demands for money at unreasonable times."[15] When one employee claimed his wages upon a chance meeting with his employer, Houck refused payment until "all facts could be more fully ascertained." The hired hand's reaction to delayed pay was to hurl a ten pound weight at Houck's head. The railroad executive's response was just as quick. "Instantly I ran my hand into my hip pocket as if to draw a revolver, although I had no weapon," Houck recalled, "and moving on the dastardly coward I threatened to kill him and he quickly ran away." As a result of this incident Houck carried a revolver as he wandered alone, on foot, or on horseback, through dense forests and uninhabited stretches of the country, because he employed "men of every character."[16]

Another choice narrative concerned an inspection visit of Wall Street financiers who were potential purchasers of Houck's unprosperous railroad. To impress "foreign" capitalists with the activity of his line, Houck refused to let the trains complete their ordinary runs. Car after car hammered over the rails, each with all the weight its engine would pull. The onlookers nodded their heads sagely and among themselves agreed to a price they considered a steal. When Houck quickly unloaded the property at their inflated figure, the former financially stricken stockholders of the line cherished the purchasers' departing whispered remark: "A prosperous corporation."[17]

Legendary stories even developed relating to the Missourian's handwriting. Always believable to possessors of college diplomas upon whose parchments appeared the illegible signature of Louis Houck, board president, was the experience of an ingenious southeast Missouri farmer.[18] Houck had once scrawled out an order to the rustic for a load of hay. As neither the farmer nor anyone else could possibly decipher the note, the message was utilized by its proud possessor as a perpetual pass on the Houck railroads. Houck never chastised the man; it was reported he only regretted never having added him to his battery of highly paid lawyers.

To the writer of an imposing array of books, an indistinct but ostentatious hand was an occupational hazard. In his early days as a journalist-historian, Houck, in order to overcome transcription difficulties, grudgingly gave way to the machine age with the first purchase of a typewriter in his city.[19] Years later he ignored the contraption in favor of his individualistic script.[20] Drafting his historical compositions first in longhand, he found it necessary to read these handwritten literary efforts to the stenographer who typed them.[21] Dictated copies were then returned to him, and recomposition laboriously imitated the first procedure. There was literal meaning in the declaration that Louis Houck "talked" history. Without such verbalization, the publication of *A History of Missouri* might well have awaited the discovery of a twentieth century Rosetta Stone on the banks of the Mississippi.

Feature sketches, as well as eulogistic obituaries, however revealing of the man, his "bootheel section," and his "show-me" state, generally omitted from the Houck saga the traditional account of home, family, politics, and religion. A fuller treatment of Louis Houck at both work and play shows him as no "dull Jack;" rather does it suggest that work *was* play to the rugged nineteenth century American.

There was even suggestion that exploitation of Missouri acreage (be it for transportation, agriculture, or state history) was for Louis Houck the realization of Russell Conwell's advice in his famous sermon, *Acres of Diamonds*.[22] Louis Houck, "on the arduous plane of things actually done," achieved his success from his own back door.

As a place from which to conduct his endeavors, Louis Houck occupied the perfect home, with the descriptive name, "Elmwood."[23] The estate was five miles west of the Mississippi River town; the Giboney home was reached by a winding driveway one mile in length. The drive was adorned on either side with majestic oaks and stately elms, and in the spring, with the pastel colors of dogwood blossoms. A majestic brick house blended into the property, a 1798 Spanish land grant assigned Alexander Giboney, Mrs. Houck's grandfather, by the Spanish King's Lieutenant Governor of Louisiana, Don Zenon Trudeau. The purchase of Louisiana by Thomas Jefferson in 1803 did not disturb the Giboney's possession, and the family title has remained unchanged the past century and a half.

Such property not only served Houck as collateral in his railroad promotions;[24] it helped to provide the literary stimulus necessary to an author. After periods of historical composition lasting from early breakfast to light noon lunch, the Missouri scribe would take a short nap followed by a hike through the family woods. The beauties of the estate, undisturbed by the frontiersman's axe, seemed to refresh Houck's enthusiasm for history of the Louisiana territory; he was ready for energetic composition the remainder of the evening.[25] When he was drafting his "Reminiscences," a trek through the Houck forests helped him recapture the physical appearance of southeast Missouri in the early era.

It takes but little imagination to picture Houck returning from his afternoon walk and composing for his state histories the following paragraph:

Missouri is a land of beauty now, but, in a state of nature, before touched, and too often defaced, by the work of man, Missouri was a terrestial paradise. Indeed, nature had done everything to make the landscape one of ravishing beauty. Nowhere else on the continent did she lavish more prodigally her charms, excelling all that the highest art of man could create, on a scale magnificent and stupendous —soaring knobs in high, grassy plateaus, through which, in deep ravines, ran crystal rivers mirroring the varied sky, lined with odorous flowers and trees, forming a natural arch, and often an enchanting *coup-d'oil* characterized the Ozark country![26]

In behalf of Houck's ever-enlarging literary efforts, a library room was provided for research. During periods of composition, dictation, and recomposition, no one was permitted to disturb the writer within this sanctuary. House servants must have been relieved when forbidden to clean the research-ladened office, for it was claimed that his library contained as many books as were included in public collections.[27] Eventually, some of the many volumes were placed in every room of the home; some books were even upon the orchestra's stage in the mansion's ballroom. Miss Idress Head, who was later the wife of the eminent American historian and founder of the Mississippi Valley Historical Association, Clarence W. Alvord, was then serving in the capacity of Houck's research assistant.[28] She has recalled that on numerous occasions when guests were invited for dinner, and a controversial subject arose, Louis Houck would dash from room to room in the huge home searching for one of his many volumes that might provide definitive answers to historical problems in question.[29]

Observing the overflow of manuscripts in the home, a reporter once provided a description of the miscellaneous arrangement:

> 'DeBow's Review' and the many volumed 'Jesuit Relations' in French and English fraternize on his shelves. A copy of 'Bossu's [*sic*] Travels' printed in 1777 and the 'Letters to the Duchess of Lesdiguieres' by Father Charlevoix, printed in 1768, are there. Bound volumes of Godey's Lady's Book and Harpers Magazine dating to the seventies range

next to a life of James Monroe dated 1820. A tome
on 'Historic Highways' stands between histories of
Illinois and Louisiana.[30]

Shelves filled with green cloth-covered books entitled
"Americana," caught the experienced newspaperman's eye.
Collections of periodicals, reports of scientific investigations,
conference programs, speeches, and historical journals, dating
from 1872 to 1920, spilled forth. It was the journalist's under-
stated conclusion that "Houck had kept abreast of a wide
range of contemporary literature, and everything he read
which interested him he preserved."[31]

When a fire destroyed part of the home in later years,
important losses listed were complete files of the *Missouri
Republican* and early Cape Girardeau newspapers.[32] Houck's
weekly habit of preserving the Sunday newspapers of London,
Washington, New York, and Philadelphia no doubt made
fire prevention in the old mansion difficult. To solve the problem of fire-proof storage, Houck finally bequeathed the
hazardous newspapers to the college whose board of regents
he served as president.[33]

As an historian, Houck was often compelled to consider
fire's dangers. He once made a gift of documents to the
Missouri Historical Society upon the condition that it obtain
a fire-proof building.[34] In his early days of traveling in New
Madrid County, Missouri, Houck had unearthed some 4,000
administrative records written in Spanish, French, and
English.[35] These had been left by the Spaniards when they
relinquished the Louisiana territory to the French at the
turn of the nineteenth century. The aspiring state chronicler
had the records copied, classified, and bound into eleven
volumes for his own research. He then returned the originals
to the New Madrid County courthouse depository, only to
witness the complete destruction by fire of the courthouse
and its contents in 1908, the year before the publication of
his state histories.

Conscious of fire's destruction, Houck demanded of his
stenographer-typist three copies of his three volumed *History
of Missouri*.[36] One he kept in his business office, one in his

library study at "Elmwood," and a third was placed in the vault of the downtown city bank. Houck never forgot the destruction of his notes when he edited the first fifteen volumes of the *Missouri Reports*. The printing offices of the *Missouri Republican* burned on May 25, 1870, and the young editor was faced with a hurried reconstruction of his legal research to meet the publication date; subsidy by the state legislature was involved.[37]

Mary Hunter Giboney, who became Mrs. Louis Houck on Christmas Day, 1872, was acknowledged to be the perfect wife for the versatile Missourian. So intensely interested was she in the early Houck railroad projects "that each morning although the weather was very cold, she climbed into her sidesaddle, mounted her favorite mare "Daisy" and rode up and down the right of way encouraging the workmen, providing them all at intervals with hot coffee and short lunches."[38]

And it was Mrs. Houck who suggested double pay to all workers on New Year's Eve in order to hasten the construction of her husband's first railroad into Cape Girardeau. Fearing that "celebrating" workmen might not be available on January 1st, she realized that the contract terms might not be met and a bonus forfeited.[39]

Also, it was Mrs. Houck who insisted that her husband draft his reminiscences so as to preserve the events of an active life for his family's sake. And it was Andrew Giboney's only child who guarded her husband's literary privacy while assuming the responsibility of a growing family of three children, Giboney, Erma, and Rebecca.[40]

Almost in the capacity of a research assistant, Mrs. Houck became acquainted with all works on Missouri history which might contain scraps of information useful to the composer of the definitive record of the state.[41] These items she collected and classified according to subject matter. It seemed most becoming that the wife of the Missouri historian was active in all local historical endeavors. She prized her membership in the Colonial Dames and the Daughters

of the American Revolution.[42] She offered prizes to the citizens
of the state for historical essays on Missouri subjects.[43] Such
activity effectively complemented the local historical chores
of her husband, who was demanding preservation of the
state's records and was bequeathing to the small towns
located on his railroad lines historic but unpronounceable
Indian names.[44] "There were a few Indians left in Southeast
Missouri when Mr. Houck began penetrating the swamp
forests," explained one newspaper, and Indian titles were af-
fixed to the railway villages because Houck "always had a
fellow feeling for the wild man."[45]

In his "Reminiscences," Louis Houck penned a conclusion that "it was impossible for me to live in a country
and become identified in its business or its people living in
it without taking an interest in its early settlement and
growth and the development of its agricultural, industrial
and social life."[46]

He might have added that it was inconceivable for him
not to impress upon his contemporaries the political views
which underscored his economic beliefs. In the Grant era,
Houck had already concluded, as had scores of the rising
business elite of the United States,[47] that being a salaried
political officer was unprofitable.[48] However, he never ceased
recommending political action he deemed advisable. This
was clearly shown via paid advertisements in the local newspapers during Houck's fight against drainage organizations
and by the political activity of his only son, who served one
term as state legislator.[49]

Although the *Cape Girardeau Democrat* stated on April
11, 1891, that "people who know Louis Houck know that he
takes less interest in the city elections in this city than any
other man who owns property here," there were important
occasions when Houck attempted to influence political decisions on the plane of state affairs. At the time Houck made
Cape Girardeau his permanent home in 1869, he was identified as a states-rights Democrat opposed to the Republican's
program of government centralization and reconstruction.[50]

Previously he had offered his speaking services to his party in its struggle to capture the southern Illinois labor vote. In a lecture delivered in 1866 before the Trades' Cooperative Union of Cairo, Illinois, Houck declared his sympathies to be with the workingman. He advocated a reduction of working hours from ten to eight so laborers would have sufficient leisure for the cultivation of the mind. Anticipating twentieth century demands of organized labor, he urged workmen to combine politically, predicting that such a labor aggregation would secure a capital as large and boundless as the capital of the largest corporation in the country. When he recommended consolidation, Louis Houck unconsciously revealed that in the future, he, as a petty capitalist, would simulate the Goulds in their manipulations as railroad overlords. Bluntly, he informed his audience:

> The interests of the working men are identical. Working men must be a unit not only in their club rooms, but a unit on every question that relates either directly or indirectly to them. Only thus can they secure political importance, make their influence felt. Let workmen be divided by immaterial 'isms,' forget their own interests, and their significance ceases at once. Unity of action gives power. Prompt demonstration of that unity on proper occasions secures respect. Think you capital is divided? Think you that one capitalist pulls one way and another capitalist in another direction? If you do, you deceive yourself. Capital is always united. It is in the nature of capital to unite.[51]

In 1894, "the indefatigable railroad builder of Southeast Missouri" represented the bootheel section at the Democratic state convention.[52] Houck, then at the high point of his legal battle with the Goulds over the control of the Cape Girardeau railroad, was excellent newspaper "copy." The impression that he was a lone individual fighting foreign capitalists for the preservation of his own identity was furnished by such convention reports as:

> W. Speed Stephens of Boonville, brother of the state treasurer and a prominent banker of Central, Missouri, received an evidence of Lewis [sic] Houck's

enmity to corporations and corporation men. Mr.
Stephens dropped into a vacant seat near Houck,
when the latter rudely exclaimed: "It's too hot to
have so many people around here. You get up and
get out of here."[53]

Interviewed prior to the opening of the assembly, Louis
Houck explained his unusual participation:

> The time has come for the Democratic Party of the
> state to take a stand against the wrongs of corpora-
> tions. If we don't do it we shall create a Populist
> movement in Missouri which will wreck our party
> here as the Republican Party was wrecked at Kan-
> sas.[54]

Obviously Louis Houck had not appeared as a radical political innovator. He was conservatively cast with the "Business
and commercial groups within the Missouri democracy" who
had absorbed the Populist silver ultimatum because "it had
a favorable monetary tradition."[55] He could utilize the Democratic convention to portray his struggle with the Goulds
in an effective state-wide manner.

An unsuccessful attempt to gain the adoption of several
resolutions "which will be something of firebrands in the
convention"[56] perhaps best explained Houck's attendance
at this political gathering. Houck's fight to reduce the maximum rates on railroads in the state was based on the assumption that farm products had decreased in price due to the
demonitization of silver. He demanded the enforcement of
a constitutional provision requiring that the different railroads of the state be treated as one in the imposition of
local rates on a shipment. Highlighting his well publicized
anti-corporation position, Houck sought a constitutional
convention for the purpose of increasing membership in the
Missouri Senate from 34 to 60. A larger body never blocked
legislation in the interests of the people, reasoned Houck,
whereas a small body was too easily controlled by the "big
boys."

Attempting to invoke a larger setting for the convention,
Houck asserted before his political brethren that matters

affecting the entire population of the trans-Mississippi country should be resolved by the adoption of free coinage of silver in the ratio of sixteen to one.[57] By driving the gold-bugs from the convention, Houck contended that "Imperial Missouri" would retain her leadership of the western states, and its delegates would prove themselves not "the tender belongings of Wall Street and New York."

Houck's failure to induce Eastern investment in his western railroad projects had shaped his politics. With his first line then in receiver's hands for failure to pay interest on its bonds, Houck found himself in a debtor's position. In the midst of panic years, the vast holder of agricultural tracts was ever mindful of the bootheel's agrarian sentiments. The prosperity of his roads, which carried the extractive agricultural type products, was affected adversely by the tight money policies of the time. Once asked how much of the freight carried on his roads was first class, Houck gave an answer which was descriptive of his section's econ-omy: "Not very much. The people don't dress as fine down there as they do elsewhere."[58] Nevertheless, Houck did not believe conditions were so bad that they called for the com-plete Populist remedies of governmental regulation and con-trol. The Democratic Party's acceptance of inflation was sufficient remedy.

Waging the war of small entrepreneur against larger corporate forces, Louis Houck played his politics believably and skillfully. As chairman of the committee on resolutions of the Cape Girardeau Democrats in 1902, Louis Houck promoted the recommendation that delegates to the state and judicial conventions deny themselves railroad passes.[59] He requested legislation imposing a $1,000 fine on any rail-road issuing a free ride to any official of the state. A fight against such resolutions by the local attorneys of the Cotton Belt and Iron Mountain railroads, W. H. Miller and J. W. Limbaugh, and D. B. Seibert, State Bank Examiner and brother of the chairman of the State Democratic Committee, quickly developed. Dramatically pointing his finger in Seibert's face, Houck charged: "I know you to be the tool and hireling of corporation interests in this state. I know you to be a paid hireling of the lobby."[60]

Seibert retorted that Houck was a liar. When Houck's son, Giboney, attempted to assault Seibert, the county meeting of the Democrats ended.

That Louis Houck was not of progressive political temperament was demonstrable when a St. Louis paper printed his interpretation of the new state primary law. Houck minced no words: the law was a delusion, ought never to have been enacted, and was only promoted by a few disgruntled office seekers from his section. To Houck this much was certain:

> A poor man under this system has about as much chance to secure a State office as a one-legged man to win a foot race with an able-bodied man. The law should have been entitled "An act to turn over the State offices of Missouri to influential aristocrats and wealthy men and keep poor men out of State offices."

Houck implied that St. Louis, Kansas City, and St. Joseph would write the state ticket for the country folks. As the primary law left "everything to chance," a junta must be formed to advise the people how to vote. To Houck, the choice lay between advice to the people from "self-constituted leaders or bosses," as the result of the present primary law, or from a convention of delegates selected in "a systematic and orderly way by the people of several townships." A state convention of delegates elected through the processes of township primaries and county conventions was, in Houck's mind, the truly representative approach. Emphatically Houck concluded, "This primary law spells disorganization and anarchy." That the Houck family was not "progressive" was shown when Giboney Houck, in his one term in the Missouri legislature, opposed women's suffrage.[62]

Years later Houck's political opinion intruded into his historical writing. In his book on the lives of southeast Missourians, he wrote that M. L. Clardy

was a leader of first importance in the political
conventions that prevailed before the present grab-
bag system of selecting candidates for official positions was adopted—a system which crowds out of
the race for promotion poor and modest and un-
assuming men, but opens the door wide to men of
wealth—and the impudent, self-seeking and loud
mouthed demagogues.[63]

Houck was unmindful of the fact that he had put a stamp
of approval upon one who had represented Missouri Pacific
interests at the time of the famous Houck-Gould litigation.
At that time Clardy had been symbolic of the corporate influence that Houck had criticized as unfairly controlling
political destinies in the state.

Louis Houck, a states rights Democrat of the 1860's,
developed a close attachment to isolationist Senator James
A. Reed of Missouri in the 1920's, and adhered to the anti-
Wilson views of the Senator who was often his guest at
"Elmwood."[64] Houck, of German descent, could probably
entertain no other viewpoint. Indicative of the nationalistic
complexities in politics, the Cape Girardeau County Democrats had found it necessary to criticize Houck's son, Giboney,
who was in the state legislature protesting against legislation
withdrawing German from the schools' curriculum.[65]

Louis Houck resembled many another businessman of
his day in his interdenominational approach towards religion.[66] He singled out no denomination as his personal choice;
he cheerfully contributed to all the churches in his community. The mayor of the city recalled that a Methodist
committee, leaving Louis Houck after final payment of a
$2,000 pledge on its church building, was met by another
delegation from another church seeking a smaller sum.[67]
According to the mayor, Houck remarked before both groups
that it would not do to have only one big church in the community. He then gave the second committee more money than
it originally sought by equating the amount with his first
gift. To the city official, this was evidence that "no man

had a greater respect for the church, although he took no part in active worship."

In the manner of a feudal baron, Louis Houck built a church on his estate for the use of his tenants. One reporter has quoted Houck's decision for such provision simply as: "Damn 'em, they need it."[68] Mrs. Alvord referred to the "joy" the Houcks shared in the supervision of the construction of the church and in the purchase of an organ.[69] As long as she acted as Mr. Houck's research assistant, Mrs. Alvord remembered the Houcks always in attendance. In addition to her research duties, Mrs. Alvord served as director of the church's choir and supervisor of the bowling alley which Louis Houck had built for his tenants to use on Sunday afternoons.

Although the Houcks were married by a Catholic priest, Louis Houck never became a Catholic.[70] When Mrs. C. W. Heil, personal secretary to Houck, chided him for not joining the Roman Catholic Church, Houck replied that if he ever found time to join a church, that would be his preference.[71]

On February 18, 1925, at the age of eighty-five, Louis Houck died of bronchial pneumonia. The day before, Houck had seemed to be improving from a cold and had personally assumed direction of the planting of additional trees on his estate.[72] With dispensation from Archbishop John J. Glennon of St. Louis, a short funeral service was conducted February 19, 1925, by the Reverend Father M. J. LeSage, pastor of Cape Girardeau's historic Catholic Church, St. Vincent's.[73]

Two months later, April 26, 1925, memorial services in honor of the late Louis Houck were held at Southeast Missouri State College.[74] Fred Naeter, owner and publisher of the *Cape Girardeau Southeast Missourian*, spoke on "Mr. Houck, the Neighbor." Houck had once encouraged the Naeter brothers in their newspaper work by lending them money for their printing offices. According to the editors, Houck "furnished every dollar [for new quarters] without a scratch of a pen to show that he was protected." The only request made by Houck was: "Promise me that you will never give any attention to any other business; that you will center your energy on this one business, that you will not buy stock in any other concern. Then there can never be any danger of my getting stuck on these notes."[75]

"This good Democrat," added the editors, "never criticized our policies even during the times we were conducting a hysterical Republican newspaper."

R. S. Douglass, local historian and dean of the college, substituting for Thomas Marshall of the Washington University history department, spoke of "Mr. Houck, the Historian." Governor Sam A. Baker of Missouri addressed the audience on "Mr. Houck, the Educator." "Mr. Houck, the Citizen" was the subject of Louis Houck's close personal friend, Senator James A. Reed.

The memorial services effectively tied together the varied interests of Louis Houck. It was as William Southern had written, that an account of the man and his activities would provide sufficient material for a "romance."[76]

Notes to Chapter VII

[1] *Missouri Republican* (St. Louis, Missouri), May 11, 1872.

[2] *St. Louis Post-Dispatch,* February 21, 1925; June 1, 1929; *St. Louis Star,* February 21, 1925.

[3] *Marble City News,* April 28, 1869, reprinted in *Cape Girardeau Democrat,* August 24, 1907.

[4] John Eddy Franklin memoirs, *The Democrat Argus* (Caruthersville, Missouri), July 14, 1946; Henry Wollman, "The Strange Story of the Cape Girardeau Railroad," *Commercial Law Journal* (June, 1933), p. 1.

[5] *Missouri Republican,* June 2, 1887.

[6] Charles and Mary Beard, *The Rise of American Civilization,* II (New York, 1927), 195.

[7] *Missouri Republican,* June 2, 1887. Also see *Statements and Testimony of Railroad Managers, of Shippers, farmers and others, taken before the Committee on Railroads and Internal Improvements of the extra session of the 34th General Assembly of Missouri* (Jefferson City, 1887), p. 352.

[8] "The Donaldson Bond and Stock Company vs. Louis Houck," *Missouri Reports,* CCXIII (1909), 429.

[9] *St. Louis Post-Dispatch,* March 1, 1925.

[10] *The Democrat Argus,* July 12, 1946.

[11] Louis Houck, "Railroad Work," I, 109.

[12] *The Democrat Argus,* July 12, 1946.

[13] R. H. Tawney, *Religion and the Rise of Capitalism.*

[14] *St. Louis Post-Dispatch,* March 1, 1925.

[15] Louis Houck, "Railroad Work," I, 25.

[16] For Houck's attitude toward labor see *Missouri Republican,* November 2, 1869.

[17] *Tiger* (Cape Girardeau, Missouri), March 28, 1941. Feature story by Ruth Anna Zoelsmann, daughter of Arnold Zoelsmann, Houck's auditor.

[18] *St. Louis Post-Dispatch,* February 21, 1925.

[19] *Ibid.,* March 1, 1925.

[20] For example of Houck's script, see signature under portrait opposite title page of *A History of Missouri,* I (Chicago, 1908).

[21] Maynard C. Willis, "Red Letter Books Relating to Missouri," *Missouri Historical Review,* XXXV (October, 1940), 84.

[22] See Merle Curti, *Growth of American Thought* (New York, 1943), p. 649.

[23] *Southeast Missourian* (Cape Girardeau, Missouri), December 21, 1944.

[24] *Weekly Republican* (Cape Girardeau, Missouri), May 28, 1915.

[25] Interview with Mrs. Christine Wheeler Heil, Cape Girardeau, Missouri, summer, 1950.

[26] Louis Houck, *A History of Missouri,* I (Chicago, 1908), 31-32.

[27] William Southern, Jr., "Louis Houck," *Cape Girardeau Southeast Missourian,* April 25, 1925. Also see *Missouri Historical Review,* II, 284.

[28] Marion Dargan, Jr., "Clarence Walworth Alvord," *The Marcus W. Jernegan Essays in American Historiography,* ed. William T. Hutchinson (1937), p. 326.

[29] Interview with Mrs. C. W. Alvord, Columbia, Missouri, fall, 1950.

[30] *St. Louis Post-Dispatch,* March 1, 1925.

[31] Interview with Miss Sadie T. Kent, librarian emerita, Kent Library, Southeast Missouri State College, spring, 1951. Working in the Houck law offices the writer noticed Houck had been a consistent clipper of materials.

[32] *Cape Girardeau Southeast Missourian,* March 30, 1918.

[33] Interview with Miss Sadie T. Kent, spring, 1951.

[34] *St. Louis Republic,* May 10, 1908.

[35] *Ibid.*

[36] Willis, p. 84.

[37] *Missouri Republican,* May 26, 1870.

[38] *Southeast Missourian,* December 21, 1944.

[39] Louis Houck, "Railroad Work," I, 33.

[40] Interviews with Mrs. Alvord and Mrs. Heil.

[41] *St. Louis Republic,* May 10, 1908.

[42] *Southeast Missourian,* December 21, 1944.

[43] *Daily Republican* (Cape Girardeau, Missouri), April 14, 1911.

[44] *Weekly Republican,* September 30, 1910; February 24, 1911; November 30, 1917.

[45] *Cape Girardeau Democrat,* July 13, 1907. Also see Mayme Lucille Hamlett, "Place Names of Six South East Counties of Missouri" (unpublished Master's thesis, University of Missouri, Columbia, Missouri, 1938), pp. 207-9.

[46] Houck, "Reminiscences," p. 264.

[47] Beard, pp. 173-5.

[48] Houck, "Reminiscences," pp. 49-50.

[49] See following issues of *Cape Girardeau Southeast Missourian*: November 1, December 20, 1918; January 3, February 7, February 14, February 21, March 21, April 11, April 25, 1919.

[50] *Missouri Republican,* October 21, 1869; Scrapbook of articles by Louis Houck [n.d., n.p.], Houck Law Offices, Cape Girardeau, Missouri.

[51] Louis Houck, *Lecture, delivered before the Trades Cooperative Union of Cairo* (Cairo, Illinois, 1866). Pamphlet of the Democratic Party of Illinois.

[52] *Cape Girardeau Democrat,* May 19, 1894.

[53] *Kansas City Daily Journal,* May 16, 1894.

[54] *St. Louis Globe-Democrat,* May 15, 1894.

[55] Donald Konold, "Silver Issue in Missouri Politics" (unpublished Master's thesis, University of Missouri, Columbia, Missouri, 1950), p. 119.

[56] *Cape Girardeau Democrat,* May 10, 1894; *Kansas City Daily Journal,* May 15, 1894.

[57] *Kansas City Daily Journal,* May 16, 1894.

[58] *Statements and Testimony of Railroad Managers,* p. 353.

[59] *Cape Girardeau Democrat,* June 6, 1902.

[60] *Ibid.*

[61] *St. Louis Republic,* August 26, 1908.

[62] *Cape Girardeau Southeast Missourian,* June 27, 1919.

[63] Louis Houck, *Memorial Sketches of Pioneers and Early Residents of Southeast Missouri* (Cape Girardeau, Missouri, 1915), pp. 100-1.

[64] *Cape Girardeau Southeast Missourian,* April 22, 1925.

[65] *Ibid.,* April 25, 1919.

[66] William T. Doherty, Jr., "Business Impact upon Protestantism," *Business History Review,* XXVIII (1954), 143.

[67] *Cape Girardeau Southeast Missourian,* February 23, 1925.

[68] *St. Louis Post-Dispatch,* March 1, 1925.

[69] Interview with Mrs. C. W. Alvord.

[70] Louis Houck, *Memorial Sketches,* p. 77.

[71] Interview with Mrs. Heil.

[72] *St. Louis Post-Dispatch,* March 1, 1925.

[73] *Cape Girardeau Southeast Missourian,* February 19, 1925.

[74] See *ibid.,* April 24, 25, 26, 27, 1925.

[75] Major Leilyn M. Young, "The Southeast Missourian and the Naeter Brothers, A study of Community Service in Cape Girardeau, Missouri, by a Newspaper and its Publishers" (unpublished Master's thesis, University of Missouri, Columbia, Missouri, 1949), p. 56.

[76] *Cape Girardeau Southeast Missourian,* April 25, 1925.

BIBLIOGRAPHY

MANUSCRIPTS

Beckwith, Thomas. "The Story of the Settlement and Settlers of Mississippi County, Missouri," edited by Louis Houck. This typewritten manuscript is located in the Kent Library of Southeast Missouri State College, Cape Girardeau, Missouri. Beckwith died in 1914, and Houck's preface and introduction to the work is dated November 24, 1917.

Houck, Louis. "Some Reminiscences of Louis Houck." This manuscript, approximately 250 pages in length, is in the possession of Major Giboney Houck, Cape Girardeau, Missouri. There are two copies, one of which Major Houck keeps at his home, "Elmwood," about five miles from Cape Girardeau, and the other one, which the writer used, is located in the Houck law offices, in downtown Cape Girardeau. The manuscript is typewritten, but the page numbers and the title page have been penciled in. In some cases repetitious material has been crossed out by pencil, and the pagination is often inaccurate. In other cases, pages have been skipped in the chronological numbering. If no page number is cited in this study, it is because of the above factors. The same is true of the manuscript below. The writer would judge that the "Reminiscences" were written in the 1910-1920 period.

————, "The Story of the Railroad Work of Louis Houck, 1880 to 1920." This manuscript is in two bound books which the writer has referred to as Volume I and Volume II. The first volume is approximately 250 pages, the second volume approximately 150 pages. These are also typewritten, with penciled title and page numbers. Volume I is concerned mainly with Louis Houck's first railroad, and Volume II with his railroad building north and south of Cape Girardeau.

————, Correspondence of. Miscellaneous, in vault in the president's office, Southeast Missouri State College, Cape Girardeau, Missouri.

FEDERAL AND STATE DOCUMENTS

A. MISSOURI SUPREME COURT CASES

"Andrew Giboney, Plaintiff in Error, vs. City of Cape Girardeau, Defendant in Error," *Missouri Reports*, LVIII, 1874, 141-5. Truman A. Post, Reporter. St. Louis: W. J. Gilbert, 1875.

"The State *ex rel.* Board of Education, Appellant, vs. the County Court of Wayne County," *Missouri Reports*, XCVIII, April term, 1889, 362-8. F. M. Brown, Reporter. Columbia, Missouri: E. W. Stephens Printing Company, 1890.

"The Cape Girardeau Southwestern Railway Company, Appellant vs. Hatton," *Missouri Reports,* CII, October term, 1890, 45-56. F. M. Brown, Reporter. Columbia, Missouri: E. W. Stephens Printing Company, 1891.

"The State *ex rel.* Klotz vs. Ross, *et al.*," *Missouri Reports,* CXVIII, November 9, 1893, 23-79. F. M. Brown, Reporter. Columbia, Missouri: E. W. Stephens Printing Company, 1894.

"The State *ex rel.* Merriam, Petitioner, vs. Ross, Judge, *et al.*," *Missouri Reports,* CXXII, June 4, 1894, 435-78. F. M. Brown, Reporter. Columbia, Missouri: E. W. Stephens Printing Company, 1895.

"William Brown Estate Company, Appellant, vs. Wayne County," *Missouri Reports,* CXXIII, June 25, 1894, 464-79. F. M. Brown, Reporter. Columbia, Missouri: E. W. Stephens Printing Company, 1895.

"The St. Louis, Cape Girardeau and Fort Smith Railway, Appellant, vs. Wayne County," *Missouri Reports,* CXXV, December 4, 1894, 351-8. F. M. Brown, Reporter. Columbia, Missouri: E. W. Stephens Printing Company, 1895.

"Merriam vs. the St. Louis, Cape Girardeau and Fort Smith Railway, *et al.,* Appellants," *Missouri Reports,* CXXVI, January 22, 1895, 445-8. F. M. Brown, Reporter. Columbia, Missouri: E. W. Stephens Printing Company, 1895.

"The State *ex rel.* Renfro, Prosecuting Attorney, vs. Wear, Judge, *et al.," Missouri Reports,* CXXIX, July 2, 1895, 619-29. F. M. Brown, Reporter. Columbia, Missouri: E. W. Stephens Printing Company, 1896.

"The St. Louis, Kennett and Southern Railroad Company, *et al.,* vs. Wear, Judge, *et al.," Missouri Reports,* CXXXV, June 30, 1896, 230-69. F. M. Brown, Reporter. Columbia, Missouri: E. W. Stephens Printing Company, 1897.

"Merriam vs. St. Louis, Cape Girardeau and Fort Smith Railway," *Missouri Reports,* CXXXVI, December 1, 1896, 145-69. F. M. Brown, Reporter. Columbia, Missouri: E. W. Stephens Printing Company, 1897.

"The State *ex rel.* Merriam vs. Ross, *et al.," Missouri Reports,* CXXXVI, December 1, 1896, 259-75. F. M. Brown, Reporter. Columbia, Missouri: E. W. Stephens Printing Company, 1897.

"The State vs. Wear," *Missouri Reports,* CXLV, June 25, 1898, 162-230. Perry S. Rader, Reporter. Columbia, Missouri: E. W. Stephens Printing Company, 1899.

"Southern Illinois and Missouri Bridge Company, Appellant, vs. Stone, *et al.," Missouri Reports,* CLXXIV, April 1, 1903, 1-53. Perry S. Rader, Reporter. Columbia, Missouri: E. W. Stephens Printing Company, 1903.

"Brooks, Appellant, vs. Schultz, Collector," *Missouri Reports,* CLXXVIII, December 9, 1903, 222-8. Perry S. Rader, Reporter. Columbia, Missouri: E. W. Stephens Printing Company, 1904.

"Southern Illinois and Missouri Bridge Company vs. Stone, *et al.,* Appellants," *Missouri Reports,* CXCIV, February 26, 1906, 175-89. Perry S. Rader, Reporter. Columbia, Missouri: E. W. Stephens Printing Company, 1906.

"The State *ex rel.* Hines, Prosecuting Attorney, vs. Cape Girardeau and Jackson Gravel Road Company," *Missouri Reports,* CCVII, November 27, 1907, 85-107. Perry S. Rader, Reporter. Columbia, Missouri: E. W. Stephens Printing Company, 1908.

"The State *ex rel.* Hines, Prosecuting Attorney, vs. Scott County Macadamized Road Company, Appellant," *Missouri Reports,* CCVII, November 6, 1907, 54-85. Perry S. Rader, Reporter. Columbia, Missouri: E. W. Stephens Printing Company, 1908.

"The Donaldson Bond and Stock Company, vs. Louis Houck," *Missouri Reports,* CCXIII, July 3, 1908, 416-41. Perry S. Rader, Reporter. Columbia, Missouri: E. W. Stephens Printing Company, 1908.

"The Cape Girardeau and Thebes Bridge Terminal Railroad Company, vs. Southern Illinois and Missouri Bridge Company," *Missouri Reports*, CCXV, December 23, 1908, 286-98. Perry S. Rader, Reporter. Columbia, Missouri: E. W. Stephens Printing Company, 1909.

"Morley and Morehouse Railroad Company, et al., Plaintiffs in Error, vs. John Himmelberger," *Missouri Reports*, CCXLVII, December 24, 1912, 179-97. Perry S. Rader, Reporter. Columbia, Missouri: E. W. Stephens Printing Company, 1913.

"Louis Houck, et al., Appellants, vs. Little River Drainage District, et al.," *Missouri Reports*, CCXLVIII, March 1, 1913, 373-94. Perry S. Rader, Reporter. Columbia, Missouri: E. W. Stephens Printing Company, 1913.

"The State ex rel. John McWilliams, Prosecuting Attorney of Scott County, Appellant, vs. Little River Drainage District, et al.," *Missouri Reports*, CCLXIX, December 21, 1916, 444-63. Perry S. Rader, Reporter. Columbia, Missouri: E. W. Stephens Printing Company, 1917.

"The State ex rel. J. Henry Caruthers, Prosecuting Attorney of Cape Girardeau County, Appellant, vs. Little River Drainage District," *Missouri Reports*, CCLXXI, July 12, 1917, 429-37. Perry S. Rader, Reporter. Columbia, Missouri: E. W. Stephens Printing Company, 1918.

B. MISSOURI COURT OF APPEALS CASES

"Louis Houck, Appellant, vs. O. C. Frisbee, Respondent," *Missouri Appeal Reports*, LXVI, March 24, 1896, 16-22. David Goldsmith, Reporter. Columbia, Missouri: E. W. Stephens Printing Company, 1896.

"Mary H. G. Houck, et al., Appellants, vs. John Patty, et al., Respondents," *Missouri Appeal Reports*, C, March 17, 1903, 302-11. M. R. Smith, Reporter. Columbia, Missouri: E. W. Stephens Printing Company, 1904.

"The Little River Drainage District, Respondent, vs. Louis Houck and Mary G. Houck, Appellants," *Missouri Appeal Reports*, CCVI, December 7, 1920, 283-7. Alphonso Howe, Reporter. Columbia, Missouri: E. W. Stephens Printing Company, 1921.

C. UNITED STATES SUPREME COURT CASES

"Missouri ex rel. Merriam vs. St. Louis, Cape Girardeau and Fort Smith Railway Company," *United States Reports*, CLVI, March 4, 1895, 478-85. J. C. Bancroft Davis, Reporter. New York: Banks Law Publishing Company, 1895.

"Stone vs. Southern Illinois and Missouri Bridge Company," *United States Reports*, CCVI, May 13, 1907, 267-75. Charles Henry Butler, Reporter. New York: Banks Law Publishing Company, 1907.

"Scott County Macadamized Road Company vs. State of Missouri ex rel. Hines, Prosecuting Attorney of Cape Girardeau County," *United States Reports*, CCXV, December 20, 1909, 336-41. Charles Henry Butler, Reporter. New York: Banks Law Publishing Company, 1910.

"Houck vs. Little River Drainage District," *United States Reports*, CCXXXIX, November 29, 1915, 254-67. Charles Henry Butler, Reporter. New York: Banks Law Publishing Company, 1916.

D. MISSOURI STATE DOCUMENTS

Journal of the House of Representatives of the 33rd General Assembly of Missouri, 1885. Jefferson City: Tribune Printing Company, 1885.

Journal of the House of Representatives of the 34th General Assembly of Missouri, 1887. Jefferson City: Tribune Publishing Company, 1887.

Journal of the House of Representatives of the 38th General Assembly of Missouri, 1895, Jefferson City: Tribune Printing Company, 1895.

Journal of the Senate of the 34th General Assembly of Missouri, 1887. Jefferson City: Tribune Printing Company, 1887.

Journal of the Senate of the 38th General Assembly of Missouri, 1895. Jefferson City: Tribune Printing Company, 1895.

Laws of the State of Missouri of the 17th General Assembly, 1853. Jefferson City: James Lusk, 1853.

Laws of the State of Missouri of the 25th General Assembly, 1870. Jefferson City: Horace Wilcox, Public Printer, 1870.

Laws of the State of Missouri of the 33rd General Assembly, 1885. Jefferson City: Tribune Printing Company, 1885.

Laws of the State of Missouri of the 34th General Assembly, 1887. Jefferson City: Tribune Printing Company, 1887.

Laws of the State of Missouri of the 38th General Assembly, 1895. Jefferson City: Tribune Printing Company, 1895.

Laws of the State of Missouri of the 41st General Assembly, 1901. Jefferson City: Tribune Printing Company, 1901.

Laws of the State of Missouri of the 45th General Assembly, 1909. Jefferson City: Tribune Printing Company, 1909.

Official Directory of Missouri, 1885. St. Louis: John J. Daly Stationery and Printing Company, 1885.

Statements and Testimony of Railroad Managers, of shippers, farmers and others taken before the Committee on Railroads and Internal Improvements of the extra session of the 34th General Assembly of Missouri, 1887. Jefferson City: Tribune Printing Company, 1887.

Report of Committee on charges against Honorable John Walker, State Auditor, together with the testimony of Witnesses, 34th General Assembly of the State of Missouri. Jefferson City: Tribune Printing Company, 1887.

Messages and Proclamations of the Governors of the State of Missouri, ed. Floyd Shoemaker, XII. Columbia, Missouri: State Historical Society of Missouri, 1930.

Combined 5th and 6th Annual Reports of the Railroad Commissioners of the State of Missouri for 1879 and 1880. Jefferson City: Tribune Printing Company, 1881.

7th Annual Report of the Railroad Commissioners of the State of Missouri for the Year Ending December 31, 1881. Jefferson City: Burch and Ferguson, State Printers, 1882.

8th Annual Report of the Railroad Commissioners of the State of Missouri for the Year Ending December 31, 1882. Jefferson City: State Journal Company, State Printers, 1883.

9th Annual Report of the Railroad Commissioners of the State of Missouri for the Year Ending December 31, 1883. Jefferson City: State Journal Company, State Printers, 1884.

10th through *13th Annual Reports of the Railroad Commissioners of the State of Missouri for the Years Ending December 31, 1884, 1885, 1886, 1887.* Jefferson City: Tribune Printing Company, 1885, 1886, 1887, 1888.

14th and *15th Annual Reports of the Railroad Commissioners of the State of Missouri for the Years Ending December 31, 1888* and *1889.* Jefferson City: Tribune Printing Company, 1890. (These two reports are bound together, but they are separately paged and indexed.)

16th through *18th Annual Reports of the Railroad and Warehouse Commissioners of the State of Missouri for the Years Ending December 31, 1890, 1891,* and *1892.* Jefferson City: Tribune Printing Company, 1892, 1893, and 1894.

19th Annual Report of the Railroad and Warehouse Commissioners of the State of Missouri for the Year Ending June 30, 1894. Jefferson City: Tribune Printing Company, 1895. (Beginning with this report the end of the fiscal year was changed to June 30. Consequently this volume contains the report for 1893 and the first half of 1894.)

20th through *37th Annual Reports of the Railroad and Warehouse Commissioners of the State of Missouri for the Years Ending June 30, 1895* through *June 30, 1912.* Jefferson City: Tribune Printing Company, 1896 through 1913.

E. ILLINOIS STATE DOCUMENTS

Journal of the Senate of the 23rd General Assembly of Illinois, 1863. Springfield, Illinois: Baker and Phillips, Printers, 1863.

18th through *19th Annual Reports of the Railroad and Warehouse Commissioners of the State of Illinois for the Years Ending June 30, 1888* and *1889.* Springfield, Illinois: Springfield Printing Company, 1889 and 1890.

20th Annual Report of the Railroad and Warehouse Commissioners of the State of Illinois for the Year Ending June 30, 1890. Springfield, Illinois: H. W. Rokker, State Printer, 1890.

F. FEDERAL DOCUMENTS

Congressional Record, 56th Congress, 1st Session, 1900-1. Washington: Government Printing Office, 1901.

Congressional Record, 56th Congress, 2nd Session, 1901. Washington: Government Printing Office, 1901.

Senate Document 373, 63rd Congress, 2nd Session, XXVI, 1913. Washington: Government Printing Office, 1914.

INTERVIEWS

Mrs. Clarence W. Alvord, research assistant to Louis Houck, former Librarian, Missouri Historical Society of St. Louis, now living in Columbia, Missouri, Fall, 1950.

Mrs. Christine Wheeler Heil, personal secretary to Louis Houck, former secretary to the Board of Regents, Southeast Missouri State College, Cape Girardeau, Missouri. Summer, 1950.

Major Giboney Houck, son of Louis Houck, Cape Girardeau, Missouri. Summer, 1950.

George and Fred Naeter, owners and publishers, *Southeast Missourian,* Cape Girardeau, Missouri. Summer, 1950.

Miss Sadie T. Kent, librarian emerita, Kent Library, Southeast Missouri State College, Cape Girardeau, Missouri. Summer, 1950.

NEWSPAPERS

Newspapers cited, unless otherwise indicated, are in the Library of the State Historical Society of Missouri at Columbia, Missouri. However, all Cape Girardeau papers with the exception of the *Cape Girardeau Democrat* and the *Cape Girardeau Morning Sun* were consulted in Cape Girardeau in the offices of Fred and George Naeter, owners and publishers of the *Southeast Missourian,* summer, 1950.

Capaha Arrow. Cape Girardeau, Missouri. Student newspaper of the Southeast Missouri State College, Cape Girardeau, Missouri, October 19, 1949.

Cape Girardeau Democrat. Cape Girardeau, Missouri, 1891-1909. Issues for 1901 are missing. This is the earliest available Cape Girardeau paper.

Cape Girardeau Morning Sun. Cape Girardeau, Missouri, the year, 1921.

Cape Girardeau News. Cape Girardeau, Missouri, October 20, 1949.

Cape Girardeau Southeast Missourian. Cape Girardeau, Missouri, March 1, 1918, through September 10, 1925.

Charleston Enterprise Courier. Charleston, Missouri, February 26, 1925.

Commercial Appeal. Memphis, Tennessee, July 18, 1950.

Daily Republican. Cape Girardeau, Missouri, October 3, 1904, through February 28, 1918.

Democrat Argus. Caruthersville, Missouri, June 14, 1946, through August 2, 1946.

Dunklin Democrat. Kennett, Missouri, April 19, 1938.

Farmington Times. Farmington, Missouri, 1910-1913.

Jefferson City Daily Tribune. Jefferson City, Missouri, selected issues, 1895-1904.

Kansas City Daily Journal. Kansas City, Missouri, May, 1894.

Missouri Republican (daily). St. Louis, Missouri, 1868-1888; from November, 1873, to December, 1874, it was known as *St. Louis Republican.*

Perry County Republican. Perryville, Missouri, 1901-1906.

St. Louis Globe-Democrat. St. Louis, Missouri, selected issues, 1890-1925.

St. Louis Home Journal and Commercial Gazette. St. Louis, Missouri, August 24, 1872.

St. Louis Post-Dispatch. St. Louis, Missouri, selected issues, 1885-1951.

St. Louis Republic. St. Louis, Missouri, 1888-1919.

St. Louis Star. St. Louis, Missouri, February 21, 1925 .

Southeast Missourian. Cape Girardeau, Missouri, September 11, 1925, through January 27, 1951.

Tiger. Cape Girardeau, Missouri. Student newspaper of Central High School, Cape Girardeau, Missouri, March 28, 1941.

Volksblatt. Belleville, Illinois, 1864 (clippings). Consulted by writer in the Houck law offices, Cape Girardeau, Missouri.

Weekly Republican. Cape Girardeau, Missouri, February 7, 1908-February 28, 1918.

ARTICLES

Alvord, Clarence W. "A Critical Analysis of the Work of Reuben Gold Thwaites," *Proceedings of the Mississippi Valley Historical Association,* ed. Benjamin F. Shambaugh, VII, (Cedar Rapids: Torch Press, 1914), 321-33.

Anonymous. "Wealthy Missourian Spends Fortune in Compiling Authentic History of State," *St. Louis Republic,* May 10, 1908.

————. "Fine Book Making at the Lakeside Press," *The Lakeside Press,* II, No. 3. (January 26, 1925).

————. "Louis Houck," *Bulletin of the Missouri Historical Society,* VII, No. 3 (June, 1950).

————. "Louis Houck," *Southeast Missouri State College Alumni Bulletin* (Cape Girardeau, Missouri, October 14-15, 1949).

Barclay, Shepard. "Memorial Sketch of Melvin L. Gray," *The Missouri Historical Society Collections,* II, No. 7 (October, 1906), 44-53.

Barclay, Thomas S. "E. A. Hitchcock," *Dictionary of American Biography,* IX, 74-75. New York: Charles Scribner's Sons, 1932.

————. "Thomas A. Sherwood," *Dictionary of American Biography,* XVII, 102-3. New York: Charles Scribner's Sons, 1935.

Beinlich, B. A. "The Latin Immigration in Illinois," *Transactions of the Illinois State Historical Society,* No. 14 (1909), 209-14.

Bek, William G. "The Followers of Duden," *The Missouri Historical Review,* XVII, No. 1 (October, 1922), 28-56.

Brennan, Frederick H. "By Louis Houck—A School, Six Books, 500 Miles of Railroad, Only Man who ever beat Jay Gould in a Deal," *St. Louis Post Dispatch,* March 1, 1925.

Carter, Clarence E. "The United States and Documentary Historical Publications," *The Mississippi Valley Historical Review,* XXV, No. 1 (June, 1938), 3-24.

Dargan, Marion, Jr. "Clarence Walworth Alvord," *The Marcus W. Jernegan Essays in American Historiography,* ed. William T. Hutchinson. Chicago: The University of Chicago Press, 1937. pp. 323-38.

Douglass, Robert Sidney. "History of the Missouri State Normal School at Cape Girardeau," *Educational Outlook* (1913-1914), I, No. 1, 20-24; I, No. 3, 144-7; I, No. 4, 214-6; II, No. 1, 3-6; II, No. 2, 58-61; II, No. 3, 158-64.

Fox, Dixon Ryan. "State History—I," *The Political Science Quarterly,* XXXVI, No. 4 (December, 1921), 572-85.

————. "State History—II," *The Political Science Quarterly,* XXXVII, No. 1 (March, 1922), 100-18.

Hinchey, Allan H. "The Commercial Club," *Educational Outlook,* I, No. 1 (April, 1913), 25-27.

Houck, Louis. "Navigable Rivers," *The American Law Review,* II (1868), 589-98.

————. "Thomas Beckwith: The Farmer-Archaeologist," *Educational Outlook,* II, No. 3 (1915), 113-22.

————. "The Story of a Raid on the Old Branch Bank of Missouri at Cape Girardeau," *The Missouri Historical Review,* XVII, No. 4 (July, 1923), 522-4.

MISSOURI HISTORIAN AND ENTREPRENEUR

Marshall, George. "Benjamin F. Yoakum," *Dictionary of American Biography,* XX, 611-612. New York: Charles Scribner's Sons, 1936.

Martin, Mrs. W. W. "Equal Suffrage and Social Welfare," *Educational Outlook,* II, No. 4 (1915), 224-36.

McHaney, Hal H. "The History of the McHaney Family in Dunklin County," *The Dunklin County Historical Society,* May 24 (1948), 317-31.

Morison, Samuel Eliot. "Faith of a Historian," *The American Historical Review,* LVI, No. 2 (January, 1951), 261-75.

Rader, Perry S. "The Great Seal of Missouri," (Part II), *The Missouri Historical Review,* XXIII, No. 2 (January, 1929), 447-62.

Randall, John Herman, Jr., and Haines, IV, George, "Controlling Assumptions in the Practice of American Historians," *Theory and Practice in Historical Study: A Report of the Committee on Historiography,* 15-52. New York: Social Science Research Council Bulletin No. 54, 1946.

Ranney, Robert G. "The City's Railroads," *The City Directory of Cape Girardeau, Missouri, for 1906,* pp. 198-206. Cape Girardeau, Missouri: Naeter Brothers, Publishers.

Read, Conyers. "The Social Responsibilities of the Historian," *The American Historical Review,* LV, No. 2 (January, 1950), 275-85.

Riegel, Robert E. "The Missouri Pacific, 1879-1900," *The Missouri Historical Review,* XVIII, No. 2 (January, 1924), 173-96.

Ross, Earle D. "A Generation of Prairie Historiography," *The Mississippi Valley Historical Review,* XXXIII, No. 3 (December, 1946), 391-410.

Villard, Oswald Garrison. "The 'Latin Peasants' of Belleville, Illinois," *Journal of the Illinois State Historical Society,* XXXV, No. 1 (March, 1942), 7-20.

Willis, Maynard C. "Red letter books relating to Missouri," *The Missouri Historical Review,* XXXV, No. 1 (October, 1940), 80-86.

Wollman, Henry. "The Strange Story of the Cape Girardeau Railroad," *Commercial Law Journal,* XXXVIII (June, 1933), 1-16.

Zoelsmann, Ruth Anna. "Our Town," *The Tiger* (Central High School, Cape Girardeau, Missouri), March 28, 1941.

REVIEWS

Review of Louis Houck's *The Law of Rivers* in the *Missouri Republican,* October 10, 1868. Article not signed.

Review of Louis Houck's *A Treatise on the Mechanics Lien Law* in *The American Law Review,* I (1867). Pages missing, due to peculiarities of the binding of old volumes.

Review of Louis Houck's *The Boundaries of the Louisiana Purchase* by Frederick W. Moore in *The American Historical Review,* VII, No. 3 (April, 1902), 607-8.

Review of Louis Houck's *A History of Missouri* by Jonas Viles in *The American Historical Review,* XIV, No. 4 (July, 1909), 834-5.

Review of Louis Houck's *A History of Missouri* in *The Missouri Historical Society Collections,* III, No. 1 (1908), 98; and III, No. 3 (1910), 313-9. Not signed.

Review of Louis Houck's *The Spanish Regime* by Isaac Joslin Cox in *The American Historical Review,* XVI, No. 1 (October, 1910), 172-3.

Review of Louis Houck's *The Spanish Regime* in *The Missouri Historical Society Collections,* III, No. 4 (1911), 449. Not signed.

Review of Louis Houck's *Memorial Sketches of Pioneers and Early Residents of Southeast Missouri* by E. M. Violette in *The Mississippi Valley Historical Review,* III, No. 3 (December, 1916), 417.

Review of Louis Houck's *Memorial Sketches of Pioneers and Early Residents of Southeast Missouri* in *The Missouri Historical Review,* X, No. 1, (October, 1915), 46. Article not signed.

SPEECHES AND ADDRESSES

Unless otherwise indicated, these speeches and addresses were found in scrapbooks in the possession of Major Giboney Houck, Cape Girardeau, Missouri.

Corleux, Mrs. F. J. "What is the History of Our City?" *Cape Girardeau Southeast Missourian,* January 26, 1925.

Houck, Louis. "The resources and future of Southeast Missouri," an address delivered at Fredericktown, Missouri, September 28, 1869.

————. "The Tendency to Centralization," an address delivered at Charleston, Missouri, July 27, 1870.

————. "The Federal Courts," an address delivered before the Missouri Bar Association, printed in the *Missouri Republican,* December 30, 1882.

————. An address delivered before the Immigration Convention at Cape Girardeau, July, 1889.

————. An address delivered at the World's Fair in Chicago, printed in *The Cape Girardeau Democrat,* September 9, 1893.

————. "Tribute to Leo Doyle," *Cape Girardeau Democrat,* February 3, 1900.

————. "In the matter of the Little River Drainage District," an address delivered at Cape Girardeau, January 19, 1911.

————. "Tribute to Alexander Buckner," printed in the *Cape Girardeau Democrat,* September 28, 1897.

————. "History of the Methodists and Protestant Religion in Missouri," an address before a Methodist Church convention in Cape Girardeau, printed in the *Daily Republican,* Cape Girardeau, September 30, 1910.

————. "Prehistoric Roads of Southeast Missouri," an address delivered at Cape Girardeau, printed in the *Daily Republican,* Cape Girardeau, February 24, 1911.

————. "Don Louis Lorimer, the founder of Cape Girardeau," an address delivered at Cape Girardeau, printed in the *Daily Republican,* Cape Girardeau, June 28, 1912.

Houser, Judge Norwin D. "Louis Houck," a speech delivered at the Homecoming Exercises of Southeast Missouri State College, Cape Girardeau, October 14-15, 1949. Issued in pamphlet form by the *Cape Girardeau News* [n.d.].

Myers, Vest C. "Louis Houck," a speech delivered before the students of Will Mayfield College [n.d.], to be found in Kent Library, Southeast Missouri State College, Cape Girardeau, Missouri.

Paar, Judge William. "How Cape Girardeau became burdened with railroad bonds," a speech delivered at Jackson, Missouri, county seat of Cape Girardeau County, printed in *Cape Girardeau Southeast Missourian,* May 16, 1919.

SPECIAL STUDIES

Adams, Charles F., Jr., and Adams, Henry. *Chapters of Erie and Other Essays.* New York: Henry Holt and Company, 1886.

Alvord, Clarence W. *The Governors Letter Books, 1818-1834.* (*Collections of the Illinois State Historical Library,* Vol. IV.) Springfield, Illinois: Illinois State Historical Library, 1909.

————. (ed.). *Kaskaskia Records, 1778-1790.* (*Collections of the Illinois State Historical Library,* Vol. V.) Springfield, Illinois: The Trustees of the Illinois State Historical Library, 1909.

————. *The Illinois Country, 1673-1818.* (*The Centennial History of Illinois,* ed. C. W. Alvord, Vol. I.) Springfield, Illinois: Illinois Centennial Commission, 1920.

Bateman, Newton, and Paul Selby. (ed.). *The Historical Encyclopedia of Illinois.* 2 vols. Chicago: Munsell Publishing Company, 1906.

Becker, Carl L. *Everyman His Own Historian.* New York: F. S. Crofts and Company, 1935.

Bek, William G. *The German Settlement Society of Philadelphia and its Colony, Hermann, Missouri.* Philadelphia: Americana Germanica Press, 1907.

Bolton, Herbert E. *Athanese de Mezieres and the Louisiana-Texas Frontier.* Cleveland: Arthur H. Clark, 1914.

Breese, Sidney. *The Early History of Illinois,* with a biographical memoir by Melville W. Fuller. Chicago: E. B. Myers and Company, 1844.

Burson, Caroline Maude. *The Stewardship of Don Esteban Miro.* New Orleans: American Printing Company, Ltd., 1940.

Carter, Clarence Edwin. "The Territory of Louisiana-Missouri, 1803-1806," (*The Territorial Papers of the United States,* Vol. XIII.) Washington: Government Printing Office, 1946.

————. "The Territory of Louisiana-Missouri, 1806-1814," (*The Territorial Papers of the United States,* Vol. XIV.) Washington: Government Printing Office, 1946.

Clevenger, Homer. "Agrarian Politics in Missouri, 1880-1896." Unpublished Doctor's dissertation, University of Missouri, 1940.

Cole, Arthur C. *The Era of the Civil War, 1848-1870.* (*The Centennial History of Illinois,* ed. C. W. Alvord, Vol. III.) Springfield, Illinois: Illinois Centennial Commission, 1919.

Conard, Howard L. (ed.). *Encyclopedia of the History of Missouri.* 6 vols. New York: Southern History Company, 1901.

Curti, Merle, and Carstensen, Vernon. *The University of Wisconsin, A History, 1848-1925,* Vol. I. Madison: The University of Wisconsin Press, 1949.

Davis, Mary F. Smyth. *History of Dunklin County, Missouri.* St. Louis: Nixon Jones Printing Company, 1895.

Douglass, Robert Sidney. *History of Southeast Missouri.* 2 vols. Chicago: Lewis Publishing Company, 1912.

Fitzsimmons, Margaret Louise. "Railroad Development in Missouri, 1860-1870." Unpublished Master's thesis, Washington University, 1931.

Gregory, Winifred, editor. *American Newspapers, 1821-1936, A Union List of Files Available in the United States and Canada.* New York: H. W. Wilson Company, 1937.

Hamlett, Mayme Lucille. "Place Names of Six Southeast Counties of Missouri." Unpublished Master's thesis, University of Missouri, 1938.

————. "Place Names of Six Counties in Southeast Missouri." Special investigation, University of Missouri, 1949.

Haupt, Hellmut Lehmann. *The Book in America.* New York: R. R. Bowker Company, 1939.

Houck, Louis. *Lecture, delivered before the Trades Co-operative Union of Cairo.* Cairo, Illinois: Democratic Company, 1866.

————. *A Treatise on the Mechanics Lien Law in the United States.* Chicago: Callaghan and Cutler, 1867.

————. *A Treatise on the law of navigable rivers.* Boston: Little Brown, and Company, 1868.

————. (ed.). *Reports of Cases argued and determined in the Supreme Court of the State of Missouri from 1835 to 1837.* 15 vols. Belleville, Illinois: Kimball and Taylor, Printers, 1870.

————. *The Boundaries of the Louisiana Purchase.* St. Louis: Phillip Roeder's Book Store, L. S. Taylor Printing Company, 1901.

————. *A History of Missouri from the earliest explorations and settlements until the admission of the state into the union.* 3 vols. Chicago: R. R. Donnelley and Sons, 1908.

————. *The Spanish Regime in Missouri; a collection of papers and documents relating to upper Louisiana principally within the present limits of Missouri during the dominion of Spain, from the Archives of the Indies at Seville, etc., translated from the original Spanish into English, and including some papers concerning the supposed grant to Colonel George Morgan at the mouth of the Ohio, found in the Congressional Library, edited and with an introduction and notes.* 2 vols. Chicago: R. R. Donnelley and Sons, 1909.

————. *Memorial Sketches of Pioneers and Early Residents of Southeast Missouri.* Cape Girardeau, Missouri: Naeter Brothers, Publishers, 1915.

Howe, M. A. DeWolfe. *J. F. Rhodes, American Historian.* New York: D. Appleton and Company, 1929.

Koerner, Gustave. *Memoirs of Gustave Koerner, 1809-1896,* ed. Thomas J. McCormack. 2 vols. Cedar Rapids: Torch Press, 1909.

Konold, Donald. "The Silver Issue in Missouri Politics." Unpublished Master's thesis, University of Missouri, 1950.

Kraus, Michael. *A History of American History.* New York: Farrar and Rinehart, 1937.

Leonard, John W. (ed.). *The Book of St. Louisans; a biographical dictionary of leading living men of the city of St. Louis.* St. Louis: The St. Louis Republic, 1912.

Lopata, Edwin L. *Local Aid to Railroads in Missouri.* New York: Columbia University Press, 1937.

Marbut, C. F. *The Evolution of the Northern Part of the Lowlands of Southeastern Missouri. (The University of Missouri Studies,* ed. Frank Thilly, I, No. 3), Columbia, Missouri: E. W. Stephens Press, 1902.

Marquis, Albert Nelson. (ed.), *Who's Who in America, 1924-1925.* Chicago: A. N. Marquis and Company, 1925.

Marshall, Thomas Maitland. *A History of the Western Boundary of the Louisiana Purchase, 1819-1841, (University of California Publications in History,* Vol. II, 1914.) Berkeley: University of California, 1914.

Miller, C. A. *The Lives of the Interstate Commerce Commissioners and the Commission's Secretaries.* Reprinted from the *Interstate Commerce Commission Practitioners Journal,* June, 1946.

Million, John W. *State Aid to Railways in Missouri.* Chicago: The University of Chicago Press, 1896.

Minnegerode, Meade. *Certain Rich Men.* New York: G. P. Putnam, 1927.

Missouri State Planning Board. *Local Road Administration in Missouri, an Interpretation in terms of its historical development.* Jefferson City, Missouri, July, 1936.

Morison, Samuel Eliot, and Commager, Henry Steele. *The Growth of the American Republic.* Vol. II. New York: Oxford University Press, 1942.

Ogilvie, J. S. *Life and Death of Jay Gould and how he made his millions.* New York: J. S. Ogilvie, 1892.

Poor, Henry Varnum. *Manual of the Railroads of the United States, Showing Their Route and Mileage; Stocks, Bonds, Debts, Cost, Traffic, Earnings, Expenses, and Dividends; Their Organizations, Directors, Officers, etc.* 14th through 57th Annual Numbers, 1881 to 1924. New York: H. V. and H. W. Poor.

Reynolds, John. *The Pioneer History of Illinois.* Belleville, Illinois: N. A. Randall, 1852.

————. *My Own Times, embracing also the History of my Life.* Belleville, Illinois: B. H. Perryman and H. L. Davison, 1855.

Riegel, Robert E. *The Story of the Western Railroads.* New York: The Macmillan Company, 1927.

Ripley, William Z. *Railroads, Rates and Regulations.* New York: Longmans, Green, and Company, 1913.

————. *Railroads, Finance and Organization.* New York: Longmans, Green, and Company, 1915.

Robertson, James Alexander. *Louisiana under the rule of Spain, France, and the United States, 1785-1807.* 2 vols. Cleveland: Arthur H. Clark, 1911.

Scharf, J. Thomas. *History of St. Louis City and County.* 2 vols. Philadelphia: L. H. Everts and Company, 1883.

Scott, F. W. *Newspapers and Periodicals of Illinois, 1814-1879. (Collections of the Illinois State Historical Library,* Vol. VI. [*Bibliographical Series,* Vol. I]). Springfield, Illinois: Illinois State Historical Library, 1910.

Shoemaker, Floyd C. *A History of the State Historical Society of Missouri, 1898-1948.* Columbia, Missouri: State Historical Society, 1948.

Thompson, James Westfall. *A History of Historical Writing.* 2 vols. New York: The Macmillan Company, 1942.

Twain, Mark. *Life on the Mississippi.* New York: The Hermitage Press, 1944.

Viles, Jonas, *et al. The University of Missouri, a Centennial History.* Columbia, Missouri: University of Missouri, 1939.

Wilgus, Curtis, editor. *Hispanic American Essays, A Memorial to James Alexander Robertson.* Chapel Hill: The University of North Carolina Press, 1942.

Willis, Maynard Cameron. "The Construction of Railroads in Southeast Missouri." Unpublished Master's thesis, University of Missouri, 1933.

Young, Major Leilyn M. "The *Southeast Missourian* and the Naeter Brothers, A Study of Community Service in Cape Girardeau, Missouri, by a newspaper and its publishers." Unpublished Master's thesis, University of Missouri, 1949.

The United States Biographical Dictionary and Portrait Gallery of Eminent and Self Made Men. Missouri volume. New York: United States Biographical Publishing Company, 1878.

The Bench and Bar of St. Louis, Kansas City, Jefferson City and other Missouri Cities. St. Louis: American Biographical Publishing Company, 1884.

History of Southeast Missouri, Embracing an Historical Account of the Counties of Ste. Genevieve, St. Francois, Perry, Cape Girardeau, Bollinger, Madison, New Madrid, Pemiscot, Dunklin, Scott, Mississippi, Stoddard, Butler, Wayne, and Iron, and Including a Department Devoted to the Preservation of Personal, Professional and Private Records. Chicago: Goodspeed Publishing Company, 1888.

The Library of Congress Catalogue of Printed Cards. 167 vols. Ann Arbor, Michigan: The Association of Research Libraries, 1942-1946.

Yearbook of the Missouri Historical Society. St. Louis: Mound City Press, 1926.

MISCELLANEOUS

Bulletins of the Little River Drainage District, No. 5, November, 1915, and No. 18, February, 1919. General Library, University of Missouri, Columbia.

11th Annual Report of the University of Wisconsin, Appendix E, Catalogue of the Officers and Students.

Rand McNally and Company's Indexed County and Township Pocket Map and Shippers Guide of Missouri for 1885. Library, State Historical Society of Missouri, Columbia.

Scrapbooks containing articles by Louis Houck, in possession of Major Giboney Houck, Cape Girardeau, Missouri.

Scrapbooks containing articles on the life and work of Louis Houck, appearing at the time of his death and at the time of the dedication of Houck Stadium, in vault in president's office, Southeast Missouri State College, Cape Girardeau, Missouri.

APPENDIX A

EARNINGS OF HOUCK'S FIRST RAILROAD†

THE CAPE GIRARDEAU ROAD

Year	Mo.'s Av. Gross Earnings Per Mile	Iron Mt. Gross Earnings Per Mile	Houck Gross Earnings Per Mile	Houck Total Passenger Earnings	Houck Total Freight Earnings	Houck Total Earnings	Houck Total Expenses	Houck Net
1881	$6,339	$10,769	$570	$5,034	$4,069	$9,103	$6,372	$2,731
1882	6,305	9,683	914	9,435	14,332	23,767	15,962	7,804
1883	6,343	8,881	836	10,747	19,041	33,456	27,135	6,320
1884	6,259	8,189	802	11,761	24,324	41,704	32,367	9,337
1885	5,917	7,926	1,793	10,640	48,028	64,005	48,490	15,515
1886	6,143	7,922	1,895	13,581	78,646	98,504	62,510	35,994
1887	6,449	7,823	2,364	13,618	102,229	122,946	68,873	54,073
1888	5,296		2,115	15,842	103,289	126,907	64,189	62,718
1889	5,963		1,461	30,092	116,090	146,182	70,075	76,107
1890	6,095	7,421						
1891	5,986	7,014	1,695	48,575	118,476	170,228	89,809	80,419
1892	6,405	7,486						
1893		6,671						
1894		$6,192	$1,304	$32,492	$87,626	$122,635	$116,124	$1,754
1895			958	20,226	70,095	99,187	85,369	6,577
1896			1,083	28,905	82,699	113,930	109,285	4,644
1897		6,196	1,203	25,126	86,021	114,143	122,781	9,637*
1898	5,591	7,082	1,267	26,966	87,694	114,661	118,098	3,437*
1899	5,741	7,255	1,091	24,154	74,119	100,815	85,390	15,425
Purchased by Southern Missouri and Arkansas								
1900	6,277		1,697	38,348	111,102	156,888	111,050	45,837
1901				33,847	150,717	208,373	121,609	86,764

*Deficit

†Information shown in Appendices A, B, and C, was obtained from *Reports of Railroad and Warehouse Commissioners of Missouri* and *Poor's Manuals of Railroads* for dates indicated.

APPENDIX B

EARNINGS OF HOUCK'S SECOND SYSTEM
ROADS SOUTH OF CAPE GIRARDEAU

Year	Mo.'s Av. Gross Earnings Per Mile	Houck Gross Earnings Per Mile	Houck Total Passenger Earnings	Houck Total Freight Earnings	Houck Total Earnings	Houck Total Expenses	Houck Net	Houck Mileage
St. Louis, Kennett and Southern								
1891	$5,986		$ 6,864	$ 19,144	$ 26,008	$ 11,130	$ 14,878	19
1898	5,591	$1,334	30,510	45,551	77,393	48,138	27,924	58
1900	6,277	1,646	40,145	67,869	110,000	68,391	41,609	58
Houck's Missouri and Arkansas								
1894	5,403	216	821	1,991	2,812	2,492	320	13
1898	5,591	341	3,006	5,591	9,557	5,960	2,696	28
1900	6,277	808	4,800	16,935	23,230	11,728	11,501	28
Cape Girardeau, Bloomfield and Southern								
1900	6,277	1,072	6,452	21,966	29,138	17,264	11,874	27
St. Louis and Gulf								
1903	7,206	2,248	65,507	336,394	428,437	289,981	138,456	190

These are the only reports turned in during this period by the various Houck companies comprising the system below Cape Girardeau.

141

APPENDIX C

EARNINGS OF HOUCK'S THIRD SYSTEM

CERTAIN ROADS NORTH OF CAPE GIRARDEAU

Year	Mo.'s Av. Gross Earnings Per Mile	Houck Gross Earnings Per Mile	Houck Total Passenger Earnings	Houck Total Freight Earnings	Houck Total Earnings	Houck Total Expenses	Houck Net	Houck Mileage
				Chester, Perryville and Ste. Genevieve				
1898	$5,591	7,082	1,267	26,966	$ 15,494	$ 16,594	$ 1,099*	19
				Chester, Perryville, Ste. Genevieve and Farmington				
1900	6,277	972	7,361	20,709	28,075	22,319		28
1903	7,206	2,041	6,470	25,046	33,820	19,722	5,756	16
1904	7,153	1,455	6,160	17,143	24,111	23,683		16
1905	7,372	1,452	5,656	17,974	24,071	22,160		16
1906		804	20,993	28,487	51,132	73,017		63
1907		1,151	21,840	40,850	64,333	85,987		63
1908		1,642	9,017	23,131	32,148	29,300		19
1909			11,657	24,877	44,353	33,163	11,190	19
1910			18,381	53,937	84,730	61,955	22,775	63
1911			19,987	57,188	106,211	66,086	40,125	63
1912			19,515	57,390	87,158	75,744	11,414	63
				Cape Girardeau and Chester				
1908	959	18,896	23,304	42,201	45,582		*	44
1909		11,657	20,962	37,188	40,489		3,301*	44

*Deficit

142

CHRONOLOGICAL TABLE OF HOUCK'S BUILDING

FIRST RAILROAD

Known as the Cape Girardeau Railway Company, the Cape Girardeau and State Line Railway Company, the Cape Girardeau Southwestern Railway Company, the St. Louis, Cape Girardeau and Fort Smith Railway Company.

1881 Cape Girardeau to Delta
1882 Delta to Lakeville
1883 Lakeville to Sturdivant
1884 Idlewild to Wappapello
1888 Wappapello to Williamsville
1889 Williamsville to Hunter
1890 Certificate of extension from Hunter to Mammoth Springs filed but not undertaken
1887 Leased the Brownwood City and Northwestern Railway Company, Brownwood to Zalma
[1893-
1896 Receivership litigation. 1899, sale of the road]

SECOND SYSTEM

St. Louis, Kennett and Southern and Allied Lines

1891 Purchase of St. Louis, Kennett and Southern, from Campbell to Kennett
1892 Incorporation of Pemiscot Railroad Company to extend line from Kennett to Caruthersville
1895 Extension from Kennett to Caruthersville, completed and Pemiscot Railroad absorbed into St. Louis, Kennett and Southern
1896 Receivership proceedings connected with above line
1897 Kennett and Osceola Railroad, from Kennett to Arbyrd
1898 Kennett and Osceola Railroad, Arbyrd to Leachville
1898 St. Francois Valley Railroad, Campbell to Caligoa
1900 Pemiscot Southern, Pascola to Deering
1901 Clarkton Branch Railroad, Gibson to Clarkton, Clarkton to Gideon and Malden, Gibson to Tallipoosa

[Other lines south of Cape Girardeau]

1893 Houck's Missouri and Arkansas, Commerce to Morley
1900 Houck's Missouri and Arkansas, Commerce to Cape Girardeau
1897 Morley and Morehouse, Morley to Morehouse
1899 St. Louis, Morehouse and Southern, Morehouse to Pascola

1898   Cape Girardeau, Bloomfield and Southern, Zalma to Bloomfield to Zeta (see Brownwood City and Northwestern Railway Company, above, in connection with first railroad)

1902   Above systems consolidated into St. Louis and Gulf

THIRD SYSTEM

1894   Incorporation of Chester, Perryville, Ste. Genevieve and Farmington Railway Company

1895   Construction of above company, Perryville to Claryville finished

1898   Receivership of above road

1898   Reorganization of the Chester, Perryville, Ste. Genevieve and Farmington Railroad Company into the Chester, Perryville, and Ste. Genevieve Railroad Company, with construction to Ste. Genevieve

1900   Organization of the St. Louis, Cape Girardeau and Southern, but no construction work done

1902   Cape Girardeau and Thebes Bridge Terminal Railroad Company, from point on Houck's Missouri and Arkansas (St. Louis and Gulf) to Thebes Bridge

1903   Extension of Cape Girardeau and Thebes Bridge Terminal Railroad Company to Cape Girardeau

1902-
1905   Cape Girardeau and Chester Railroad

1904-
1913   Saline Valley Railroad, to Farmington

1913   Above systems consolidated into Cape Girardeau Northern

MISCELLANEOUS

1873   Cape Girardeau and Scott County Macadamized Road extended from Scott County to Cape Girardeau

1891-
1892   Promotion of the Grand Tower and Cape Girardeau Railroad Company of Illinois

1911   Cape Girardeau, Charleston, and Hickman Railroad Company organized but never built

INDEX

ABOUT THE AUTHOR

W<small>ILLIAM</small> T. D<small>OHERTY</small>, J<small>R</small>., is professor of history and chairman of the Department of History at the University of Mississippi, and has taught at the University of Missouri, Christian College, Westminster College, and the University of Arkansas. He received the B.A. and B.S. degrees from Southeast Missouri State College, the M.A. degree from the American University in Washington, D. C., and the Ph.D. degree from the University of Missouri.

The present study originated as Professor Doherty's doctoral dissertation. A grant from the Faculty Research Committee of the University of Mississippi, in 1958, made possible further study and the completion of the manuscript.

Professor Doherty has published several articles in *The Business History Review* of the Harvard Graduate School of Business Administration and is a member of several professional historical societies.